Development without Dependence

Pierre Uri

foreword by
William P. Bundy

Published for the
Atlantic Institute for
International Affairs

The Praeger Special Studies program—utilizing the most modern and efficient book production techniques and a selective worldwide distribution network—makes available to the academic, government, and business communities significant, timely research in U.S. and international economic, social, and political development.

Development without Dependence

PRAEGER SPECIAL STUDIES IN INTERNATIONAL ECONOMICS AND DEVELOPMENT

Praeger Publishers   New York   Washington   London

Library of Congress Cataloging in Publication Data

Uri, Pierre.
    Development without dependence.

    (Praeger special studies in international economics
and development)
    Translation of Développement sans dépendance.
    "Published for the Atlantic Institute for International
Affairs."
    Includes index.
    1. Underdeveloped areas.   2. Economic development.
3. International finance.   I. Atlantic Institute for Inter-
national Affairs.   II. Title.
HC59.7.U7713   382.1   75-19829
ISBN 0-275-55830-4
ISBN 0-275-89470-3 student ed.

PRAEGER PUBLISHERS
111 Fourth Avenue, New York, N.Y. 10003, U.S.A.

Published in the United States of America in 1976
by Praeger Publishers, Inc.

Printed in the United States of America

FOREWORD
William P. Bundy

In the small company of world-class economists, Pierre Uri has long occupied an assured and special place. Early in the postwar period, after having played a leading part in establishing a national accounts and budgeting system for his own France, he turned his attention to the economic integration of Europe. As close colleague to Jean Monnet, he was involved successively in the creation of the Schuman Plan for a European Coal and Steel Community, as economic director of that community, and as one of the key draftsmen, at the elbow of Paul Henri Spaak of Belgium, in what became the Rome agreements for the formation of the present European Common Market. "A volcano of ideas, a brilliant writer.... No progress was made when he was absent"—so says a biography of Monnet.*

Always a searcher for new frontiers, Uri naturally extended his interests in the 1960s to the problems of the world economy, and especially those of the poor countries. In 1962, he became counsellor of studies with the Atlantic Institute for International Affairs, located in Paris, and from this base served on ad hoc committees for the Alliance for Progress in 1962-63, as codirector of a 1970 mission to Asia, and most recently, in 1973, as vicepresident of the United Nations Groups of Eminent Persons dealing with the problem of multinational (or transnational) corporations. In 1974 Pierre Uri was appointed to the Economic and Social Council, the highest French constitutional body of its sort. To his friends, these honors and responsibilities have left no discernible imprint— his hair remains unmanageable, his pipe consumes the breath not needed for waves of Gallic eloquence, and the "volcano of ideas" erupts at frequent intervals.

As this book attests. In the fall of 1975, the American government —through Secretary Kissinger and Ambassador Moynihan—made at the United Nations a set of proposals designed at least to start a serious dialogue going between the developed nations of the "North" and the

---

*Merry and Serge Bromberger, *Jean Monnet and the United States of Europe* (New York: Coward-McCann, 1969), p. 159.

William P. Bundy is editor of *Foreign Affairs,* and Member of the Board of Governors, the Atlantic Institute for International Affairs.

developing nations of the "South." But Pierre Uri, along with a handful of other Western economists, had for years been following both the growing stridency of Third World demands and the evolution of a set of practical issues shrieking for, if not solutions, at least more measured and constructive action. The foreign aid programs of the 1950s and 1960s—which Pierre Uri chews to bits in this book for total lopsidedness and failure to address the needs of the truly poor—have at their best met only fractions of the total problem of the growing gap between the rich and poor nations of the world, a gap that I hope most Americans would join with Uri in thinking both inhumane and gravely threatening to world peace. Today, he argues that an effective transfer of resources and skill remains a vital part of the need, but that such nation-to-nation aid—if it lacks the framework of a basic overall approach and way of thinking—can only help to foster the very feelings of dependence ("dependencia" as the phrase originated in Latin America) that are perhaps the deepest grievance of the developing world.

It is to such an overall approach, then, that this book is chiefly directed. And while its author would be the first to disclaim neat blueprints of final answers, in this reader's judgment the book sets up more of the right headings, asks more of the right questions, and throws more light (in a relatively short space) on these headings and questions than almost anything else that the lay reader can readily grasp. Can the developed countries maintain, in the face of the crisis of energy prices, that growth that is as indispensable to the poor countries as to them? Can population growth somehow be controlled, and if not how great a drag will it be? What is the role and necessary scale of official foreign aid, especially to the neglected poorest countries? How can raw materials markets be stabilized to the benefit of both producers and consumers? What kinds of industries should the developing countries seek to build up as part of a rational world division of labor, and how can the transition be helped and at the same time made bearable for the workers in the developed countries?

The reader will find stimulating chapters on all these questions. In addition, as a special by-product of Pierre Uri's work as UN "eminent person," the two chapters on the multinational corporation contain particularly meaty suggestions on the detailed questions of control and regulation that are arising today; accepting multinational corporations as both inevitable (at this economic stage at least) and as potential engines for rapid advance, Uri also wants to see them not only unable to take advantage of national weaknesses (in particular, fairly taxed on all their operations) but also in the end contributors to employment and equity of income wherever they operate.

And lastly, thinking back to his own experience in Europe, Uri examines the extent to which regional cooperation can be developed in other areas, especially in Latin America where its promise and problems may both be greatest. While obviously hoping that such cooperation can become stronger within the regions of the deveoping world, the author is at pains to reject the idea of special ties between groups in the North and South—between the United States and Latin America, between Europe and Africa, or between Japan and East Asia. On these points, as throughout, Pierre Uri remains in essence a believer in free markets and in the kind of regulation and overall framework that release human talents and energies to the maximum.

In sponsoring this book, the Atlantic Institute for International Affairs continues its policy of the past decade, especially under the Directorship of John W. Tuthill, of devoting a major share of its research and publication effort to the relationship of the highly industrialized states with those nations and regions, mostly to the south, that are seeking to improve the welfare of their peoples. In his capacity as counsellor of studies at the institute, Pierre Uri has written himself on Latin America, edited a 1971 Institute book, *Trade and Investment Policies for the Seventies,* and participated actively in an institute project that produced in 1973 *Latin America: A Broader World Role,* by A. Krieger-Vasena and J. Pazos, with the aid of an advisory panel whose views were included. While the present book doubtless reflects the fruits of these activities, it is entirely the personal inspiration and effort of its author. The members of the Board of Governors of the Atlantic Institute have not reviewed the analysis or conclusions of the book from the standpoint of whether they agreed or disagreed with them; rather the sole criterion for institute sponsorship is that the book be a substantial and reasoned contribution to thought and action on important matters within the sphere of the institute's concerns. The responsibility for the views expressed remains that of Pierre Uri; the responsibility for their impact is the reader's.

CONTENTS

LIST OF TABLES AND FIGURES

LIST OF ABBREVIATIONS

ADELA   Association for the Development of Latin America

DAC   Development Aid Committee

ECLA   Economic Commission for Latin America

EEC   European Economic Community

GATT   General Agreement on Tariffs and Trade

GNP   Gross national product

IMF   International Monetary Fund

LDC   Less developed country

MNE   Multinational enterprise

OECD   Organization for Economic Cooperation and Development

UNCTAD   United Nations Conference on Trade and Development

Development without Dependence

CHAPTER

1

THE SHATTERED BLOC

Is the relationship of dependence between the Third World and the industrialized countries being reversed? The Third World needed their aid, their techniques, their products and even, often unwillingly, their enterprises, to develop its resources and its industries. Will they, on the contrary, now find that employment and growth are subject to the uncertain supplies of raw materials and energy which are drawn from the Third World?

The picture is not so simple. Among the industrialized countries, the two largest powers are also among the principal producers of raw materials. The United States and the USSR have vast resources of primary materials and energy—so, of course, have Canada and Australia. Dependence on external sources for the very foundations of industry happen to be the common lot of Western Europe and Japan. Hence the extraordinary reversals we have witnessed in their balance of payments and exchange rates. When there were no obstacles to the growth of industry, Europe and Japan, by importing at low prices, were able to develop their competitive capacities. In one year the American deficit reached the unheard-of figure of $30 billion. The dollar's parity vis-a-vis the deutsche mark melted away. All of a sudden entirely different perspectives brought about an abrupt rise in the American currency, later to be followed by a downfall and a new upswing, and caused fluctuations in the yen, the pound, the lira, and the franc. Each of the industrialized entities is going to find itself in radically different circumstances when it comes to offering aid or finding new markets.

Among the Third World countries, change has been no less dramatic. To identify them as primary producers, as buyers of manufactured goods, the prices of which rose higher than those of what they sell, was from

1

the start a misleading oversimplification. In times of poor harvests the rise in wheat prices was a boon to the modern farmer and a tragic load to those countries already plagued by hunger. The heaviest burden for the greater part of the Third World today arises from the steep rise in the price of oil, and perhaps also from that of some raw materials which come from other parts of the Third World. The poorest may no longer have the means to feed themselves.

Alongside this gulf between the industrialized and developing worlds another has been created, the gulf between the countries which have the rare commodities and energy, and those who must buy them. Unless one can devise brand-new mechanisms, there will be an even greater lack of means to avoid the deepening predicament of the poorer countries. This is especially true since the reform of the international monetary system, no sooner begun, has already completely changed its aims. The reform was intended to reabsorb the dollars accumulated by Europe and Japan, to substitute an international unit for the U.S. currency's former reserve role, and to create some indirect limits to large and sudden short-term capital movements between industrialized countries. We are suddenly confronted with the possibility that world reserves will be absorbed by the oil producing countries and, hence, with redoubtable alternative: either the mobility of their liquid assets will reach proportions hitherto unknown, or the accumulation will be such that they will lose all incentive to produce. The rest of the Third World would then have to suffer the effects, not only of a letup of its own growth, but also of halted growth in the industrialized world.

ONE OR SEVERAL CHASMS?

One may ask oneself why the world has waited so long to appreciate the dimensions of the predicament in which large parts of most continents find themselves. We used to speak of "new" countries—a strange term to use when almost all of these, such as China, Egypt, India, Iran, Cambodia, and Peru, have conserved admirable remains of the world's oldest civilizations. We have also spoken of "backward" countries—the term sounds very scornful, for some of these countries, by the wisdom of their ways of life, have perhaps already found answers to some of the problems the West is having to face. Over time terminology became more ponderous—underdeveloped countries soon found themselves euphemistically labelled "developing countries." These expressions will remain meaningless unless they reflect an attempt to understand the plight of these countries in real terms, on the basis of figures; without such an effort, no action can be effective.

But after all, when it comes to industrialized countries, general ignorance has been no less great. Strangely enough, the concept of national product or national income, discovered at the end of the eighteenth century, was practically lost for 150 years. The absence of any overall measurement may explain the amazing delusion through which Germany thought itself capable of conquering the world, and the Japan of the 1940s of attacking the United States. The awareness of the conditions of growth and of the different rates of development coincided with the introduction of national accounting as a means of evaluating performance and of guiding action. Per capita income provided a simple criterion for appraising the gap between the few industrialized countries and the great mass of poor countries.

The awareness of the gap has led to a twofold awakening. Foreign aid has become for the richer countries an explicit obligation, one to which they have not dared object, although their aid has in fact tended to decrease in spite of their lip service to human solidarity. It was at the Bandung Conference in April 1955 that the Asian and African countries burst forth as a power able to challenge the established state of affairs. And as the old colonialism was coming to an end, whether through military or peaceful processes, a special kind of aid began to flow from the embryonic European Economic Community (EEC) to the African countries. Latin America saw to it that U.S. promises of financial support, however ambiguous, were written into the Alliance for Progress. Would these scattered advantages break the newfound unity of the Third World?

Unity was restored with the preparation of the first session of the United Nations Conference on Trade and Development (UNCTAD), in Geneva in 1964. Raul Prebisch, the secretary general of UNCTAD, had, in a broad document, outlined the key problems and suggested new solutions. Even if one disagrees with some of his analyses or feels that other solutions might have been more effective, international thinking about development did receive a fresh impetus. The disagreements created by the Europeans' preferential treatment of African exports were overcome by the idea of generalized preferences to be accorded by all industrialized countries to all the developing ones. From then on, the 77 developing nations acted as a bloc. They lined up again at New Delhi in 1968 and numbered 95 when they met thereafter at Santiago, amounting to 110 by 1975.

But history does not repeat itself; ideas and methods must always be renewed. The abovementioned group of 77, by increasing their demands, had to face serious resistance from the industrialized countries. The New Delhi conference produced few results and, predictably enough, the same strategy led to the same disappointment at the third conference, held at Santiago in 1972. The group of 77 presented their long list of requirements;

the industrialized countries banded together to say no. What little satisfaction the Third World could glean from the Santiago conference was limited to the creation of a committee of twenty, in which some of the underdeveloped states could participate in discussions on international monetary reform. This forum replaced the group of ten, where only major financial powers were represented. The UNCTAD talks progressed slowly and world events, namely the oil crisis, soon caused all the proposals to be shelved.

In the meantime, the developed countries, particularly the two main protagonists, the United States and the EEC, and also Japan, negotiated reciprocal reductions of tariffs among themselves. Whatever advantages resulted therefrom for some of the underdeveloped countries were merely accidental by-products. For a long time the world's monetary problems had been dealt with by the group of ten, with the International Monetary Fund (IMF) acting as little more than a registry office. The drifting apart has not stopped, though the limited preferences granted by the EEC, preferences also agreed on but not ratified by the United States, do mean a gesture towards easier imports from the Third World.

Thus a basic question arises. Even before the abrupt rise in oil prices was to enrich some Third World countries and impoverish others, was it not likely that the simplistic dichotomy which had characterized relations between the developed and underdeveloped worlds for the twenty years between 1950 and 1970 and stimulated some action would begin to prove a considerable obstacle?

Failure to distinguish between widely different situations leads to a lumping together through which troublesome events occurring in one corner of the world distort the image of other countries or other regions. The disillusionment experienced in giving foreign aid to one country can lead some to want to deny it to all countries, even those whose need is greatest. The international negotiations of the 1970s show how a simple idea, which is useful at the outset, can, over time, turn out to be quite counter-productive. All the arguments for shading the dividing line, for finding a greater continuity, suddenly spring to mind. What sense is there in lumping together hitherto unknown tribes still living in the Stone Age, and the urban complex of Sao Paulo? Where does one place some of the European countries which border on the Mediterranean?—with the underdeveloped countries, or in the other bloc which culminates in the United States? There is a whole range of intermediate situations. Within the same part of the world one finds a much greater gap between Haiti and Argentina than between the latter and North America. No sooner has one discovered the concept of per capita income than one becomes aware of its limitations. Prices and ways of life differ so much that no such figures can be accepted uncritically. To allocate $50 per capita and per year in certain countries may be to disregard the base cost of the number of calories without which the population would not even survive. If Singapore claims only a $700 yearly income per person, but if local prices are three or five times lower than those in the United States or France, one should rather compare its standard of living with that of Paris, that is to say, with one of the highest in the world, to appreciate it in real terms. Fortunately new international studies are underway to bring some meaning to these comparisons. They take into account the enormous differences in price and, for the developing countries, the significance of economic activity unrelated to market transactions. Should other indicators be introduced?—for instance, the small share of manufacturing in production as a whole—in a country as prosperous as New Zealand, it is just as small—or the importance of primary products, agriculture, and raw materials in the exports of the countries concerned; it is of the highest importance in the U.S. sales abroad.

Yet, to retain only these economic criteria, themselves very difficult to figure accurately, would be to ignore more basic realities. The maintenance of traditional social structures, or political instability, strivings toward democracy, or successions of dictatorships is no less important in differentiating those countries that we call underdeveloped.

These obvious facts are not enumerated simply for the fun of upsetting conventional wisdom. Recognition of disparities not only between countries but even within each country, goes some way in explaining where there are limits to aid policies. Foreign aid is decreasing everywhere. This is not only because it had been previously stimulated by the Cold War. Indeed, the stake which both camps had in the Third World had more often than not led to the most amazing distortions in assistance programs. Furthermore, in their turn, the more advanced nations have discovered their own internal disparities, that is to say, their own islands of poverty. This more acute preoccupation has become one of the most serious obstacles to responding to aid requests from other countries.

Let us not be misunderstood. There is no question of underestimating the appalling misery which plagues the greater part of the world—but one must recognize that the methods which, up to now, have been used to fight against it, have had built-in limitations. The fact that the world's conscience has suddenly discovered the abyss that separates a small number of industrialized countries from a mass of wretched peoples is an international event which has not been without effect. However, if it were to persist in this simplified form, it cannot but result in keeping up misunderstanding and in creating new confrontations. No program of action will be effective unless it is adjusted to suit the individual differences of each continent, each country, and even each region within the larger countries.

A NEW FRAMEWORK FOR ACTION

Does this mean that the framework to be used is the same as the one already solidly implanted?—that in which each of the industrialized countries, or each group of them, concentrates on one of the underdeveloped regions, not only in the granting of aid but also in directing its investments, and even in granting preferential access to its market. This is, in fact, the worst of all possible solutions.

It can be seen in the too exclusive dialogue between the United States and Latin America. Whatever the intentions of the founders of the Alliance for Progress, the outcome was bound to give rise only to resentment and bitterness on both sides. The debate became all the more impassioned as it was directed in each case against a neighbor. It is in Latin America that the concept of *dependencia* was forged. All possible evils are heaped upon the heads of the industrialized countries. If they extract raw materials and, in their view, thereby provide the producers with the means of paying for their imports, they are accused of exploitation if not of outright plundering. If they develop local industry, then they are reproached for imposing their goods and patterns on others, for destroying local customs and traditions, for splitting societies in two—between the privileged classes who take sides with the industrialized world and the mass of the forgotten men.

The ambiguous relations which France has established with its former colonies provide us with another example in this context. There is not one African state which has not, after only a few years, asked that the terms of aid and development agreements linking it to the former metropole be changed. Privileged relations have often turned into conflicts. Even Japan, having barely begun to invest abroad, has already come up against violent reaction: little wonder, as most of this investment is directed to regions of Asia which Japan had once subjected to brutal military dominance.

There is a lesson for the EEC in all this. Its relations with the associated countries have seemed more harmonious up to now. They at least have the advantage of being doubly multilateral: the member states negotiate as a body with a group of associated states. But the aid which is thus given, constitutes only a small fraction of the combined gross national product (GNP) of the contributing countries. The EEC has for too long expected preferential treatment for its exports in exchange for the free access to its markets which it reserves for the associated countries. In the long run this road is a dangerous one for Africa, in that it leaves it increasingly at the mercy of the goodwill or the lust for power of Europe.

New ways must, therefore, be found. As an example let us start with Latin America. Europe and Japan have carefully avoided any involvement here. Except for some business relationships and even some fruitful investment, despite some visits by heads of state or government and a few newly fashioned links with the EEC notwithstanding, it can be said that in political terms, Latin America has been left to its own devices, or to those of the inter-American group—which fortunately now includes Canada. There would be a fundamental change, however, if Europe, Japan, and—why not?—the socialist countries made it possible for Latin America to intensify and diversify its relations with the industrialized world. Latin America, instead of laying the blame for all its difficulties (increasingly) on the doorstep of the United States, would become conscious of all the possibilities open to it. Within a network of multiple relations, Latin America could discover its own identity as well as its potential contribution to world affairs.

This idea can be applied more generally. There is still time, for example, to prevent Japan from finding itself alone is Asia, to imagine forms of cooperation and investment where Japan could be associated not only with the receiving countries but also with a less suspect Europe or a more distant America. Japan could, at the same time, diversify the thrust of its external activities, join European efforts in Africa, while Europe would become aware of its worldwide responsibilities and cease to neglect Asia and Latin America. This sort of trend might bring a new tone to relations between developed and underdeveloped countries, as well as among the underdeveloped countries themselves.

The difficulty is that it is not enough for aid and financial assistance to take multilateral forms. The American administration decided to make an effort to have a larger part of its external aid pass through international organizations, the World Bank group in particular. The idea was that this would lead at least to an economy of means. It would reduce the number of overseas missions and all the reports which in each country accumulate and contradict each other. But this is not enough to get around the main obstacle. Let there be no illusions on this point. The conditions generally being demanded of a developing country in exchange for the granting of financial assistance are considerably more severe than those asked of a powerful and developed country. Compare, for example, the way in which Europe gave unlimited credit to the United States, absorbing its dollars without even demanding guarantees, without laying down conditions about internal measures or balance of payments; and the careful negotiations conducted by the IMF or the World Bank for the granting of short-term credits or long-term loans to developing countries. The fact is that according to their statutes, those institutions must deal with individual countries in which—whether one likes to admit it or not—one may not have confidence.

This raises a perpetual dilemma. How many of the governments convey a sufficiently satisfactory image of competence and honesty? How many regimes, on the contrary, seem inefficient, corrupt, oppressive? Does the choice then boil down to supporting governments one disapproves of or to abandoning their populations?

Development will always be limited and precarious unless it can escape from the feeling of dependence or relationships based thereon. As long as governments in power or their oppositions can continue to lay the blame on others, the efforts made by peoples to help themselves will be constantly checked and challenged. Feelings of dependence and the situations they create can be reduced only by an entirely new approach which will deal with issues rather than with countries.

The first condition is that aid meets definite objectives and is part of a general plan. The aid must cover the basic needs of subsistence and health where production can not yet meet these needs. It must also lay the foundations for all productive investment. In other words, it must be part of an assistance program, on the one hand, and, on the other, part of a regional development policy on a worldwide scale. The rest must be provided by other means. Thus, aid programs remain more necessary than ever. But there is no doubt that they must form part of an entirely new and much wider approach to the problems of development.

This book does not presume to deal with all aspects of development.* Others have done so with a breadth, vigor, and competence and even a sympathy to which we must pay tribute. The aims in this instance are more limited and perhaps of a more immediate application.

This book proposes to outline an approach to the world's problems which might, at the same time, hasten and reform development efforts. It has as a first premise that all such efforts must aim at a few crucial points which, in turn, will have their effect on the problems as a whole. This assumes, of course, that whatever is done will be related to the current realities.

To begin with, one must measure the impact of the rise in the price of energy on the growth and the situations of the different industrialized markets. One must also have some idea as to whether the population explosion will in fact dash all hopes of development from the start.

Thereupon, one can then examine new formulas for financing and distributing aid. The rapid increase of international investment, especially through multinational corporations, is an undeniable fact. Some rules or

---

*On the problems of education, see Ladislav Cerych, *Aid to Education* (Atlantic Institute, 1965); on inflation and the means of combating it, see Pierre Uri, Nicholas Kaldor, Richard Ruggles, and Robert Triffin, *A Monetary Policy for Latin America* (Atlantic Institute and Praeger, 1966).

mechanisms must be found, however, to maximize and conserve its advantages while eliminating its ill-effects as much as possible.

The abrupt rise in the price of oil and some other raw materials has accentuated the already fairly evident split between the different parts of the Third World—as regards the level of income and the rate of growth. Some developing countries have suddenly become richer, others poorer. This is due less to world inflation and its effect on industrial prices than to the rise in the cost of their imports from other developing countries. This situation calls for a fresh analysis of the terms of trade. It should not be impossible to link the long-awaited reform of the monetary system to a more effective stabilization of the markets for primary products.

Industrialization is, of course, an inevitable phase of development without which there would not be enough employment for a growing population. Can such a phase really be successful, however, without a reform of the measures through which industrialized countries close their markets to the very products they have financed?

Finally, developing countries will not be able to increase their bargaining power nor will they be able to attract the investments they desire, without having to make costly concessions, unless they manage to get together, so as to direct their largest industries towards enlarged markets.

Such is the sequence of chapters and proposals in this book. The aim is to examine how the obstacles may be overcome so that each country may make the best of the opportunities open to it and to substitute a common interest for the feelings of dependence and situations of confrontation. This amounts to enlisting economic devices for the achievement of political goals.

AN URGENT APPEAL

Opening new prospects for cooperation, outlining new plans of action, is inseparable from an expression of anguish and indignation. Many of these countries which know so well how to display solidarity when it comes to demanding concessions from the industrialized states, nonetheless often withdraw into themselves and cope with their own conflicts, whether latent or violent, in a manner evoking the darkest chapters of European history. Not one of these countries, with its pressing needs for resource investment, fails to overburden its budget, its production, and its balance of payments in order to arm itself. Armed forces, often ridiculously inadequate for protecting external security, are always strong enough to impose their laws and oppress the local citizenry. While military regimes spread over Latin America as they do in Africa, the industrialized countries, otherwise so miserly with their assistance and so jealous of their influence, wage the most ruthless competition to sell their instruments of destruction, oppression, and death. Beset by precarious trade balances, the countries of the East and West vie with each other all the more for this type of market. The United States has once again overtaken the Soviet Union for first place in this race; Great Britain and France are struggling for third place. Whenever a conflict breaks out, the sources of the arms of both camps become obvious—they are often the same. Each uses the same justification: why refuse to sell arms when the "others" are always ready to do so? The situation is bitterly ironical: since so many of these conflicts are fanned by sales of arms, which then are used up and replaced, would it not be all the easier to impose cease-fires since the same nations control the supply of equipment, spare parts, and munitions for all parties to the conflict? When will this deadly game end? When will the developing countries realize that warlike nationalism and prestigious war machines only serve to make them more dependent on the advanced countries which dominate the arms market? This sort of appeal, for all its obvious good sense, is so wide of the mark that it appears the blindest utopianism. And yet, if there is to be development without dependence, the world will have to move toward a twofold, though difficult, kind of agreement. The underdeveloped countries will have to agree to settle their differences peacefully, and the industrialized countries will have to renounce their dishonorable arms traffic.

2

PRICES AND GROWTH

As of 1975 it is no longer possible to conceive of a development policy without taking a gamble. Furthermore, the risk will have to be reassessed at each step. Once growth slows down in the industrialized countries, it will become obvious how erroneous the usual discussions have been. All the stress was laid on the widening of the gap between developed and underdeveloped countries. Even if their rates of growth had become comparable, the differences between them, in absolute terms, would not have ceased to increase. Once the privileged countries begin to stagnate, the repercussions on the poorer ones will create a far more serious situation. Improving the lot of the have-nots is more important than any comparison with the situation of the haves.

If, however, the prices of raw materials, energy, and even food products insofar as they come from the Third World, begin a sustained rise, everything is changed. Under those circumstances, just as with the oil-rich countries, certain poor countries would become rich. All the conventional ideas on the need for aid and industrialization would quickly become irrelevant.

Is the world at a turning point? Will the rich countries have to undertake an agonizing reappraisal of their old familiar ways, or is the oil crisis simply a passing one and are all the extrapolations we have made from it about to be contradicted, just as the idea of a perennial American surplus or a perennial American deficit have been contradicted one after another? This is not to say that the Western world should return to its old line. If, however, it is to make some basic changes in its model of civilization, it might not be the effect of a constraint but of a deliberate choice.

The obligation to search patiently for new answers to these questions cannot be avoided. Neither the different industrialized countries, nor the different developing countries, nor yet their products, can be said to be in comparable situations. In order to measure the diversity of the advantages and the risks in each case, one must look at the variety of products and distinguish between the long and the short term. As for the repercussions, one may deduce them with some degree of probability. For the industrialized countries, this will depend on their structures; for the developing ones, on their sources of supply and types of outlet.

ENERGY AND RAW MATERIALS

Will other raw materials follow the path that energy has taken? Will they be drawn this way by an imitation process, and even more so, because of the direct link between costs and the indirect link between the forces which govern the markets for all these products?

It is easy to understand that, for the long term, there is a correlation between the cost of energy and that of raw materials, the very extraction of which requires energy. Energy remains the only true bottleneck of a lasting nature, since it is the indispensable complement to all production. Perhaps only steel is comparable by the extent of its application and by the extent of its impact, for steel is used in all machines and even in the production of energy itself. Nevertheless, the growth of the demand for steel does not seem to be without limit. In relation to overall production, it is restricted by the growing importance of services. Moreover, aluminum and concrete compete, in certain circumstances, with steel. Other materials have more specialized applications.

In the short term, that is to say, in a predetermined structure, any material can constitute a bottleneck; even those which are used in only small quantities, provided they are an indispensable part of certain products or an irreplaceable element of their quality. Either these products end up fulfilling the demand or substitutes are found and in the very long term, a shortage of raw materials could only come about as a result of a shortage of energy. There are unlimited resources of titanium in seawater, of aluminum in clay, and of copper in granite; it would, however, require unlimited amounts of energy at unbelievably low cost to make their extraction economically feasible.

As it is, this correlation between the prices of energy and raw materials must be modified by another consideration. Let us take aluminum, for instance, the production of which is based essentially on electricity. If the price of energy rises too suddenly, the demand for aluminum could decline and even though the cost of extracting bauxite increases, its price could drop through this decreased demand. In other words, there is a backlash effect of factors affecting the demand for any finished product on its various ingredients.

This remark puts us on the scent of a very important correlation. The different elements which explain the fluctuations of primary products will be reviewed in detail at a later stage. It will be seen that the laws which govern these fluctuations vary according to whether the products are agricultural or nonagricultural, foodstuffs or not, whether they are also found in the main consumer societies or almost totally imported by them. Without coming to grips immediately with this analysis, one should under-line one piece of evidence which was brought to light by the abrupt rise in prices in 1972 and 1973. The industrialized countries managed to synchronize the ups and downs of their economic activity, thereby eliminating the lags which had existed among them before and which had been responsible for certain stabilizing effects. This convergence not only contributed to the acceleration of inflation but demand for industrial raw materials grew. It seems that production adapts to this rise less quickly than industry itself, where employment and working hours can be increased and where there are always certain reserves of productivity. On the other hand, a slowdown in industry can cause a sudden slackening off in the raw materials market, where production is both difficult to check or to increase; hence, the abruptness of fluctuations.

Had a production cut in oil supplies actually taken place, the repercussions on the major industrialized countries would have been dramatic. There has certainly been a slowdown in the increase of supplies and an enormous rise in price. While production on the whole has not been radically affected, it is hard to imagine that certain strategic sectors will not suffer. This is particularly the case for the automobile industry with all of its ramifications. In the short term, therefore, the rise in the price of oil may cause the prices of other industrial raw materials to fall. It is true that in the case of some natural products which had been partially replaced by oil derivatives, there will be a renewed demand. Rubber and natural textile fibers should so benefit, happily for Malaysia, Argentina, and certain African countries. Where other raw materials are concerned, the results could be quite different in the short term.

NEW DIRECTIONS FOR GROWTH

This is not an excuse for jumping to conclusions about the curbing of growth. It is strange that public opinion and indeed governments can be so unaware of the actual impact of raw materials and energy in the overall costs of production. Where raw materials are concerned, foodstuffs which are almost all processed—be it basically as wheat by the miller or meat by the butcher—must be considered separately. In fact, only fruits and vegetables are consumed "as is," even if a certain quantity is preserved. Primary foodstuffs represent some 10 percent of the GNP in industrialized countries. Other materials represent less than 5 percent or even as little as 2 percent in the United States. Moreover, the United States only imports a fraction of this 2 percent. Even in France, where dependence on oil imports is much greater than in Britain or Germany, only 2 percent of the GNP went to such purchases. The place of energy in the overall basic costs of the industrialized countries was on the order of 6 percent or 7 percent. This does not refer to raw petroleum, but to refined oil products and electricity as it is delivered to the consumer. There is a considerable difference between the cost of primary sources of energy and the cost of gasoline or electric current as and where they are finally consumed. And this very incidence of energy on total costs of production, as far as can be judged from the figures for the last two years (1959 and 1965) for which input-output tables were available, seemed to be on the wane in the United States as in Europe. A rise in the import prices does not necessarily lead to a rise in consumption costs of useable energy, greater than the absolute value of the import price increase.

In other words, the idea of radical changes in the rhythm of growth or in the structures of production must be approached with caution. The usual reasoning, and often that of economists as well, tends to exaggerate the reactions of demand to prices. What is much more important is the reaction of demand to the increase or diminution of income. The consumption of paper, aluminum, and electricity has always doubled in under ten years. Is it a fact that this consumption must diminish because of rising costs? The prices of beauticians' services or of doctors' care have not ceased to rise in comparison with other prices, and yet these services are increasingly in demand. Prophecies about slower growth due to a rise in costs, about dramatic changes in structure due to a rise in the price of energy, do not take into account certain constants which are more important as determining factors than prices are.

OIL PRICE VARIABLES

Moreover, will the price of oil necessarily continue its present upward spiral? On the one hand, we have the answer of the oil companies: The need for supplies exists—it can only grow—and producing countries have formed a monopoly. Nothing will curb their demands until a substitute is found for the energy they have for sale. There will be no limit to the rise for a number of years to come, for, as far as the nuclear option goes, it takes five years to build a plant.

The North Sea is a promising source of energy, but at best it can only supply 20 percent of Europe's future consumption. American coal reserves represent more than the whole of the world's oil reserves, but it will take time to begin to exploit them, to invest in transport by rail or to develop in situ gasification processes on a large scale. The oil reserves around the Orinoco, in South America, promise to be richer than those of all of Arabia —but the cost price is in no way comparable. Siberia is, to be sure, fabulously rich in oil and gas, but American techniques would be required to exploit them. The USSR insists that all financing be done by the future users themselves—it is not even prepared to reduce their risks to the extent of giving them the results of their geological research.

Seen in this perspective, as of 1975, the world would continue to be at the mercy of the Arabs for another ten years, or seven or eight at least.

Perhaps a more inclusive view could provide us with another answer. As of 1975, a kilowatt hour produced by nuclear energy costs half of one produced by oil. The as-yet-unexploited American coal reserves are expected to be incredibly cheap. It is not only effective competition that must be reckoned with, but potential competition as well. If the rise in the price of oil continues, and indeed accelerates, it is easy to imagine that research programs for finding other sources of energy will be embarked upon with much greater vigor, and will assume a new and greater importance. Economists and others who formulate policy in the Arab countries must realize that the greater the rise in price, the harder will be a possible fall. Even now, Saudi Arabia is calling for a reduction in price.

But the variety of conditions in these countries means that any reduction is a serious problem. Iran, Algeria, and Iraq have large populations, ambitious plans for development, and not inexhaustible sources of oil. They are tempted to take the highest price immediately and to convert their receipts into massive investments which will permit them to build up their industries and even, in the case of Iran, to build up a nuclear power base against the day when the oil reserves will have been exhausted. It is true that the discovery of a large gas field puts off this day and transforms the plans for a nuclear power base into a prestige goal rather than a necessity. But even sparsely populated countries like Saudi Arabia can make large-scale plans for the development of oil-based industries including oil refineries as well as petrochemical plants and even iron smelting. The absorption capacity of the oil producing countries would then grow rapidly, but never to the extent necessary, if the prices remain so high that their effective surplus each year continues in the vicinity of $70 billion.

Unless they know what to do with this surplus, the producers might be tempted once again to cut oil supplies. As long as energy policies and replacement energy are not available, growth in the developed countries will be severely perturbed. The needs of the poorest countries will once again take second place, and the whole world will feel the catastrophic effects.

If those responsible for the financial affairs of the Western world did not display such unbelievable sluggishness, the well thought-out economic calculation to which the advisors to Arab producers have become accustomed may show us a way out. The producing countries are already looking ahead to the day when their reserves will be exhausted. If they want to continue their economic growth, they will have to profit from the present state of affairs in order to acquire assets of a permanent kind. This being the case, they will have to take some important decisions. To keep the oil in the ground, at no interest, is a safe investment as long as prices continue to rise. At the same time, a more rational use of energy and more active research for other forms of energy will eventually bring a halt to a long-term rise. On the other hand, to acquire land in industrialized countries, land which will appreciate more rapidly and more securely, to participate in growth activities, to contribute to the reanimation of the financial market, means to become equipped with durable resources which will pay for imports of equipment long after oil ceases to be such an exceptional resource.

But there seems to be a limit to the number of transfers of this kind that are acceptable to the industrialized countries themselves. There is a dire need for assets of a new kind which could provide their holders with certain assurances without creating all kinds of stresses or conflicts.

Scarcely anything has been done up to now; hence an increase in the risks. The enormous deficits on one side are, of course, made up for by the surplus on the other. There is a sort of law of conservation in financial matters just as in physics. Surplus countries can, of course, absorb dollars, gold, or credits by lending their money; but to be useful, their loans must take a form allowing them to be absorbed by the international structures. However, the oil producers' preference for liquid assets is such that they invest most of their money in the Eurodollar market—the total amount has reached an unprecedented high, close to $200 billion—but the terms of these investments become shorter and shorter, on a weekly basis, and even in some cases, from day to day. Of course, national banking systems and even the international market have become quite used to this kind of intermediation, that is to say, short-term borrowing in order to make long-term loans. Within each country the risks of the operation are limited; if the depositors were suddenly to withdraw their money, the banks could turn to the central bank which would substitute its notes for the deposits.

There exists no similar guarantee on the international market. Banks are beginning to feel alarmed by the inflation of the deposits they receive, their disproportion to the banks' own resources, and by the growing gap between the periods for which the money is lent and the periods for which they are expected to commit themselves. This would not be the case if international monetary negotiations had not been marking time, if the promises for constructing a European monetary union had not remained purely verbal.

The situation is serious. Neither the overall deficit of the industrialized countries nor the accumulated deficit of those countries of the Third World which have not benefited from the price rises have yet revealed the full extent of the problem. To present a consolidated account for the countries of the Organization of Economic Cooperation and Development (OECD) is like saying that the American balance and the German surplus can be deducted from the deficits of Great Britain, France, or even Italy. This is far from a true picture. As Italy sees its debts growing ever larger, its capacity for borrowing becomes more and more questionable and it begins to apply restrictions; its suppliers are consequently affected and their deficits are enlarged—hence the risk of a chain reaction.

The only way to get around the problem is by the countries with a balance or a surplus being willing to lend to the others without limit. This is all the more true as the countries in surplus are the ones which naturally attract the liquid assets of the oil producers. As their needs are less great, they offer greater security for the investments. But this kind of dependence of country upon country may create unbearable political tensions.

Why does Europe hesitate to borrow in common, or to create immediately a unit of account as stable as the average of currencies within the European Community, or even as stable as the most valued among them? It could thereby quickly develop an extraordinary capacity for absorbing long-term investments coming from the oil producers. It would avoid the constant risks involved in switches from one currency to another; it would substitute its aggregate creditworthiness for the vacillating credit of some of the members of the community, each of which could then borrow from the community instead of feeling dependent on one or another of its partners. On the international level, it is easy to see that the time is not yet ripe for a genuine monetary reform, but at least one might define what future drawing rights will mean. Will it be an abstract monetary unit or a basket of currencies of countries representing more than 1 percent of world trade? It matters little one way or the other. The latter course has been chosen. The decision could furnish the model for a unit which might serve in the transactions involving investments from the great surpluses of a small number of countries.

These are the conditions for avoiding a great crisis and pursuing growth. If the banking system stopped absorbing so many highly volatile liquid assets, imports could not be maintained, production would slump, and unemployment would go out of control. Everything can be set back on the right course, provided some basic decisions are made. Indeed, even a general recovery could take place very quickly. Let the Europeans and the international market create interest-bearing stocks and shares guaranteed against monetary depreciation, and before long these will be more profitable than oil whose prices will eventually stop rising. Better still, the producers, tempted by this arbitrage, would be led immediately to place greater quantities of oil on the market, not only to acquire equipment but also the means of assuring future payments. The tendency of gradually declining prices would not wait for the development of nuclear energy, the American oil shale, or the gasification of coal. The capacity to provide aid to developing countries and the means of financing it would thus not be jeopardized at a time when it becomes more necessary than ever.

3

POPULATION AND
DEVELOPMENT

Can we assume that the situation is not hopeless from the start? It is incredible that it should have taken the world so long to perceive the predicament that its galloping demographic rate was creating. Even worse, for a long time the main concern of the population front in each country seemed to be its rate of decline in relation to others. France was worried by its altered position in Europe since the Napoleonic era when France had still boasted a population that was equal to that of Russia and almost twice that of England. It is not so long ago that eminent demographers regarded demographic growth as a major factor in economic growth. The idea was in fact primarily of military relevance. In the days of infantry, a large population meant mastery on the battlefields. Unfortunately, this way of looking at things is still not outmoded. India at the time of partition no doubt considered its gigantic population an asset in any future conflict with Pakistan. Even China has, at times, been tempted to let its enormous population grow further. Only in a world truly at peace will such a disastrous approach disappear.

When, in the past, one did worry about population growth, it was in terms of density per country. Japan and the Netherlands got a lot of attention on that score. Such observations ignored the fact, of course, that the greater a country's agricultural base, the more land it needs. The enormous growth of industrial activity has meant unprecedented economic growth for those two countries in particular, despite their high population density. Moreover, density has little meaning unless one considers what part of a country's territory is in fact inhabitable or arable. Egypt has only 23 inhabitants per square kilometer (59 per square mile); however, the greater part of the country is desert; in the narrow corridor irrigated by the Nile, the population density is 950 per square kilometer (2,430 per square mile).

Yet, today our approach has reached the opposite extreme: "Let's stop demographic growth right away, otherwise the growth of our economies will be doomed by the exhaustion of our natural resources." The more fanatical ecologists add that it should begin with a complete halt in developed countries because that is where most natural resources are consumed. Unfortunately, that is the easiest part; we're practically there. In the developed areas, Europe, the USSR, Japan, North America, temperate South America, Australia, and New Zealand, populations have grown by no more than 1 percent on the average, between 1960 and 1970. The lowest growth rate was in Europe (0.5 percent to 1 percent) and the highest, owing largely to immigration, in New Zealand and Australia. The underdeveloped world has twice that rate; the lowest is in China, where it may yet go down to 1.2 percent before the end of the century. However, in the tropical parts of South and Central America, in North Africa, in all of black Africa, in Asia outside of China and above all, in India, Bangladesh, and Indonesia, the rate is 3 percent and sometimes even higher.

For the planet as a whole, the rate of growth has been of shattering proportions. Until the beginning of the eighteenth century the world's population doubled probably no more often than every 1000 years. It increased by half between 1800 and 1950. But at the present rate, instead of every 1000 years, it would double every 35 years. From nearly 4 billion now, the world population would be up to 6 billion by the end of the century and, according to the least pessimistic of estimates, at least 11, more likely 12 billion by the beginning of the twenty-second century.

DIVERGENT VIEWS OF GOVERNMENTS

The United Nations has done some research into how countries view their own population problems and what their policies are for coping with them. Unfortunately, the answers they got to the first question were much more numerous than to the second.

Of the 148 countries which responded to the U.N. inquiry, 45 still consider their birth rate too low, 55 deem it adequate, and 48 find it excessive. The latter, however, represent 59 percent of the world's population and 81 percent of that of the underdeveloped world. Thus an effective policy on their part would have repercussions on world trends as a whole. Global population growth would be reduced to 1.7 percent by 1985, instead of 1.9 percent as is expected. It would be 2 percent rather than 2.3 percent in the underdeveloped world.

Most countries today are in favor of family planning; this includes those who do not wish to reduce their birth rates as well as those who see it as a matter of priority. A clear distinction seems to have been established between family planning and demographic planning. The first merely implies giving each household the means to have no more than the number of children it wishes; the second means it is up to the policy makers to orient economic, social, and cultural conditions in order that they can influence the number of children a family desires. As to the means, there is only a small number of countries left where modern contraceptive methods are prohibited. On the other hand, there are only 23 countries where abortion is legal or even facilitated. Most countries are, of course, mainly concerned by natural population growth; very few have deliberate policies on emigration or immigration. In fact the latter is usually discouraged, with notable exceptions such as New Zealand, Australia, Argentina, and under certain conditions, several European countries—the difference here being that the European countries prefer immigrants on a temporary rather than a permanent basis.

What is most striking is that the judgments of governments on the insufficiency or excessiveness of births in their countries are not based on the actual fertility rate. In other words, this question remains a highly subjective and national one, which only increases the difficulty of formulating a comprehensive policy.

While few countries answered questions in this area, even fewer still have taken a firm stand. In this regard, there seem to be important distinctions between continents. Fortunately, it is in the more overpopulated of them where the desire to check population growth is most evident, that is to say, in Asia. From Iran to the Philippines, governments are ready to reduce the birth rates; but it is well known that these efforts have come up against ancient traditions, especially in the larger countries where the situation is most serious, India, Pakistan, Bangladesh, Indonesia. In Africa, Egypt, Tunisia, and Kenya are aiming to reduce the number of births. In Latin America, however grave the situation might be, only some small countries of Central America in addition to Colombia, and probably soon Mexico, too, have a clear position in favor of reduced population growth. In Chile, Peru, and Uruguay, where the rates of population growth have leveled off by themselves, the governments have no plans to intervene. While several European countries, where demographic growth is, generally speaking, the lowest, are worried about their congested cities, no direct government intervention is planned. Certain countries, having known between the wars or thereafter a decline in their populations, even have a policy of encouraging births: France and Greece and, in the Communist bloc, Czechoslovakia, Hungary, and Romania, are among these.

All this means that a policy on a world scale would have to be very complex indeed. Tendencies are not the same everywhere and the imbalance between the rich and poor areas is much more serious than the overall population growth. Above all, a reasonable agreement cannot come about without a recognition of the reciprocal relationship between a moderation of population growth and an acceleration of development. This is not only the Russian and Chinese position, but also is the only one which is acceptable to the Third World.

Against this troubled and complex backdrop two propositions meet and clash. The first insists that development will remain impossible as long as the population goes unchecked. To the Third World this sounds very much like preaching by the industrialized countries. The other proposition is that development alone can bring about the kind of changes in social and cultural environments which will help to moderate population growth. It is easy to see that action on both of these fronts is necessary if the world is to master the problem of population growth. But first it is important to understand what has been happening and why it will take so long to stop it.

MORTALITY AND FECUNDITY

The key phenomenon in the nineteenth and twentieth centuries has been the lowering of the death rate; in other words, the raising of the average life expectancy. This has had its effect on the birth rate, by allowing an ever greater number of women to live until the end of their fertile period. This explains what we may call demographic inertia. The increase in life expectancy is spreading from country to country. The births of a greater number of women who will live longer results, after a certain number of years, in new increases in the birth rate. Historical experience has, however, brought to light a compensating factor. As people live longer and as parents realize that they can count on the survival of more of their offspring, there is a natural tendency to have fewer children; in fact there have been examples in certain European countries between the wars where this led to an absolute decrease in population. This compensation between the death and birth rates does not become apparent immediately; there is always a lag, the extent of which depends on the societies and times involved. It does lead to a basic understanding of demographic transition. In other words the growth trend of a population does not indefinitely follow an upward curve; after a period of expansion, which can be very long and very rapid, it tends to level off and find a new stability. The aims of a worldwide demographic policy would be to attain in each part of the world, as soon as possible, a stable level with a low death rate and a moderate birth rate.

Demographic research has clarified certain fundamental concepts by describing the different variables and their interrelations. Life expectancy at birth sums up the death rate at different ages in a given society. What lowers it most is the scale of infant mortality—those deaths which occur in the first year of life. The gross rate of reproduction conveys the fertility characteristics of a society; it complies with the number of children that would be born if the women of child-bearing age lived long enough. What is apparent in this is the net rate of reproduction, which is reduced in relation to the gross rate insofar as there is premature mortality among women. A society's population replaces itself exactly when there are, on average, two children per couple.

Until the end of the nineteenth century, the death rate in the under-developed countries was such that in spite of a high fertility rate, the populations remained, roughly speaking, more or less stagnant. On the other hand, in the developed world, the increase in life expectancy and a delay in the compensatory decline in the birth rate made for a moderate upward trend in population. This situation has now been reversed. Life expectancy, though it remains much lower in most developing countries, has been increasing at a more rapid rate, or rather over a shorter period of time than it has in the advanced countries. It is this fact and also the increased net rate of reproduction which are directly responsible for the enormous growth in the population of the Third World. It is difficult to know, considering the very short period for which prime indicators are available, whether a lowering of the birth rate will begin to compensate for the increased life expectancy or whether, as has happened in certain industrialized countries, this decrease will be only a fluctuation and not a definite tendency.

The Swedish experience provides the best demographic statistics gathered over the longest period of time; it also provides some idea of what developments and uncertainties may be involved. From the end of the eighteenth century the life expectancy in Sweden was higher than in any other country—36 years. It grew slowly and surely until the 1960s when it had doubled. Since then the progress has continued, but very slowly. In other developed countries, too, it is obvious that the causes of premature death have diminished, especially among infants by the reduction of infectious diseases. Yet, on the other hand, the development of certain kinds of cancer and cardiovascular disease, which could be the price of accelerated urbanization, suggests that life expectancy on the whole might have reached a ceiling and could even decline.

Thus, there are three phases in the decline of mortality—first a slow increase in life expectancy, then an accelerated phase, and finally a flattening out curve. The example of Mauritius, which has good statistics, makes this acceleration apparent. Life expectancy there has gone from 33 years in 1942-46 to 51 years in 1951-53, and to 60 years in 1961-63. An average of 27 years of life were added in only twenty years. The same increase took one hundred and twenty-five years in Sweden, from 1800 to 1925. Certain of the developing countries, such as Costa Rica, Mexico, Hong Kong, and Sri Lanka have made great strides in this area. This goes to show that special efforts in the field of hygiene and of social security are more effective for this kind of fundamental human progress, compared with other indices of development. Most of the Third World countries are in the second phase, that in which life expectancy increases rapidly but has not yet reached that of the advanced countries. Certain African countries are still in the first phase; but even there a first generalization is possible, which helps to reduce long-term uncertainties on evolution. The increase in life expectancy is a tendency which is spreading progressively and which will soon become general.

One of the major elements in population growth, and perhaps the most spectacular, has been the decline of infant mortality. Here again, there is a difference between the developing and the advanced countries. The lowest rate, fewer than 12 deaths per 1,000 live births, is to be found in the Netherlands, Sweden, and Finland. In other developed countries the rate is between 12 and 30. In the underdeveloped countries, the spread is much wider—fewer than 20 per 1,000 in Hong Kong and Singapore, more than 200 in some African and Asian countries, probably an average of 140 for the least developed regions as a whole. It would seem that there has been more progress in reducing the mortality of adults than that of infants. Improvements in hygiene are, in fact, not enough; it is the low level of development, the malnutrition, and the miserable housing that still constitute the greatest obstacles.

As the average life span increases, the fertility curve continues to climb in the first phase of economic progress. To come back to the example of Sweden, the curve climbed until the first third of the nineteenth century, decreased slowly and irregularly until 1890, much more rapidly up to the 1930s and during the Great Depression went below the level required to keep the population constant. In the same way, fluctuations were observed in America and France during the depression. There was an increase in births everywhere between 1945 and 1960, then followed by a decline. No such acceleration is to be seen in the Eastern European countries or those of southern Europe, in the first case because economic fluctuations are kept to a minimum, and in the other because there is a generally low awareness of these fluctuations. Thus the main difficulty is in estimating the trend of fertility in developing countries. The tendency to a decline has scarcely begun and could be reversed. In any case, the high rate of births which has obtained up to now will combine its effects with those of a lower death rate. Soon larger generations will be at the procreative age and greater numbers of women will live to the end of their child-bearing years.

It is not easy to pinpoint the connection between the level of development and the decline of fertility which tends to compensate for a higher life expectancy. In France this trend began at the beginning of the nineteenth century when the country was scarcely urbanized or industrialized. England waited until the 1890s to begin a decline, at which time already 70 percent of the population was urban and 80 percent of the male employment was nonagricultural. In more recent times, it is interesting to examine the contrasting examples of Bulgaria and Venezuela. In the first, fertility declined from 1910 on, when the population was still 80 percent rural, when 70 percent of male employment was in agriculture, when 60 percent of the adults were illiterate, and when the infant mortality rate was 60 per 1,000. On the other hand, Venezuela, despite its showing many indices of a comparatively advanced stage, still maintains a high fertility rate. Lower rates of fertility in the cities than in the country are not true everywhere, and industrialization itself has less effect than increased female employment. In other words, cultural trends matter more than economic ones. A deliberate and collective will to reduce the birth rate has often preceded any government action or has been independent of it; it has at times even gone in the face of religious pressures. Nor did it wait for modern methods of contraception.

The decline in the death rate has helped—parents need fewer children to provide them with security in their old age. However, quite understandably, the awareness that many children can be a burden rather than an asset has been late in coming. This illustrates one of the vicious circles of development; in the poorer countries resources are lacking to provide enough work for the male population, let alone for a growth in female employment which could benefit the population as a whole.

In all countries the number of births outside marriage make up but a small fraction of the total. Thus the ways in which fertility declines are to be found either in a lower marriage rate or lower fertility rates within marriages. Increased celibacy limited the birth rate in certain European countries during the nineteenth century and does so today in Argentina as well as in the USSR. Women in Europe have tended to marry later. A delay in marriage has also been observed in Singapore and appears to be a deliberate policy in China. The basic phenomenon in industrialized societies in not the will to have no children at all, but rather a reduction of the number of children per family. Couples generally have all the children they are going to have in the first years of marriage, then they stop. Whereas in the underdeveloped countries, where birth rates have not begun to fall, births continue throughout all the women's child-bearing years.

DEMOGRAPHIC INERTIA

This explains why it is so difficult to obtain rapid results in slowing down population growth deliberately. With a decline in mortality, the replacement rate itself goes up, that is, where two parents have two children. Let us take the example of North Africa; one study tried to consider the conditions which would create a balance between low rates of fertility and mortality, between 1975 and the year 2000. It was envisaged that life expectancy would rise from 50 to 70 years, that the gross rate of reproduction, that is to say, the fertility of women, would fall from 3.2 to 1.1. The population would not, however, become stable before 2075, by which time it would have tripled, going from 75 million in 1965 to more than 220 million. In India, to stabilize the population would require that the birth rate fall from 5.5, which was the case between 1965 and 1970, to only 1.1 during the period 2005-2010. Suddenly there would be very small generations, and one of two things would happen: either the population would decrease and its structure alter completely, or the birth rate would have to increase suddenly to offset the death rate. In demography, as in agricultural markets, there is always a delay before production catches up. Births lead to a wave of births 15, 20, or 30 years later. These delays can produce great fluctuations, the whole structure of employment and education could be thrown into confusion.

In any case, on a worldwide scale it will require one century before the population is stabilized, but before then there will have been an incredible redistribution between continents. Table 1 shows population figures for 1975 and 2075, divided among eight large regions in absolute numbers, as percentages of world population and in proportion to area (per square kilometer).

In one hundred years, the world's population, which is almost equally divided between north and south, will be only 30 percent in the northern hemisphere as against 70 percent in the southern hemisphere. Europe, which now has the highest population density, will be surpassed by southern Asia which will have more inhabitants than the whole world does today!

However, even as the growth of the world's population has been accelerating in the twentieth century, there no longer exists what was a common solution in the nineteenth century—international migrations. These reached vast proportions then. They populated North America and a good part of Latin America, though it is true that most of them came from Europe. Today there are only two countries, both of them very small, where the population is mainly increased by immigration: Israel and Kuwait. The United States still receives the greatest number of immigrants,

TABLE 1

World Population: Evolution and Distribution

Regions	Number of Inhabitants (in millions)		Percentage		Density	
	1975	2075	1975	2075	1975	2075
World total	3,639	12,347	100.0	100.0	29	87
Northern group	1,863	3,559	49.4	29.3	33	59
North America	228	448	6.0	3.7	11	21
Europe	462	698	11.9	5.8	97	142
Soviet Union	243	445	6.4	3.7	11	20
Eastern Asia	930	1,968	25.1	16.2	86	168
Southern group	1,776	8,788	50.6	70.7	26	109
Latin America	283	1,609	8.1	13.0	16	77
Africa	344	2,338	9.8	18.4	13	74
South Asia	1,126	4,784	32.2	38.8	66	240
Oceania	23	57	0.5	0.5	3	7

Source: UNESCO Courier, May 1974.

27

in absolute terms, that is, not as a percentage of the total population. In two large industrialized countries of Europe (the German Federal Republic and France), manpower is in good part provided by foreign labor; two smaller countries (Switzerland and Luxembourg) also count on foreigners. And, at the other side of the globe, Australia and New Zealand still have a net inflow of population. Seen on a worldwide scale, these movements are absolutely marginal; they hardly affect a million people per year, whereas the world's population increases by almost three inhabitants per second, 80 million people per year—enough people to populate six or seven cities the size of New York, Tokyo, or Shanghai, a yearly increase which is greater than the whole populations of all but six countries in the world today.

Geographic and Age Structure

The effect of this demographic growth is one of constant change on the structures of populations. While international migrations have dwindled, internal migrations have become more usual and numerous. This is particularly true of the developed countries where the rural areas have been depopulated; cities grow to populations of 100,000, 1 million and soon more than 10 million. Their overcrowding and pollution will not cease to attract attention. The same tendency is to be found in the developing countries. Their rural populations continue to grow in absolute numbers, but their percentage decreases. It has been predicted that between 1970 and 2000 there will be an increase of 64 percent in the urban populations of the developed countries and of 240 percent in the developing countries. However, in the industrialized countries, this movement to the cities follows the creation of new jobs. The tragedy of underdevelopment is that the problems of employing people productively on the land are compounded by open or disguised unemployment in the cities and the miserable living conditions in the shantytowns on their outskirts.

Another transformation in structure relates to the proportions of the different age groups. Children under 15 years of age represent less than 27 percent of the total population in the developed countries and more than 41 percent in the underdeveloped ones. People over 65 represent 10 percent in the first case and scarcely 3 percent in the second, but the latter is expected to rise to 5 percent by the year 2000. Consequently, people of working age constitute nearly two-thirds of the population in the developed countries, but not much more than half of that of the less advanced areas. It would require a very optimistic theory indeed to see this proportion raised to 60 percent by 2000.

Yet the working population, including women, and actual employment are two entirely different things. The rate of dependence is defined by the number of inactive persons who are in the care of 100 active persons. The discrepancy between developed and underdeveloped countries is even more dramatic than in the case of those parts of the populations which can not yet work or can no longer do so. In 1970 the index was 162 in the least advanced regions, compared with 123 in the most developed; for children under 15 years, 103 as against 57—for people of working age but dependent, 53 as against 46. On the other hand, owing to an unequal life expectancy there are only 6 percent of dependent old people as against 20 percent in the industrialized world. Still, in economic terms, the contrast is even greater. In the developed countries, production is not stopped by limited resources, save during exceptional periods of shortage. To be sure, there as anywhere else, the working population, in relation to the population as a whole, contributes to determining the level of living. But insofar as a check on growth can come from reduced demand, consumers who are not themselves producers enlarge the market and thus contribute indirectly to growth. In the underdeveloped countries, resources govern everything, including employment. There is, unfortunately, nothing to make up for the harsh law that the smaller a working population is in relation to the whole, the poorer everybody is.

Impact of Trend on Population Planning

The trend seems to be towards a relative decrease of those under 15 years of age and towards a small increase in the numbers of those over 65 years, between now and the year 2000. But in absolute terms the young continue to increase at a tremendous pace. The consequences thereof at the bottom and at the top of the population pyramid are not the same, nor are the measures to be taken. To raise life expectancy is, of course, an unquestionable priority. If the number of old people increases, there will be that many more mouths to feed; food and consumer goods will simply have to be further divided. Greater security for old people can, however, have a salutary effect on the population movement, as it diminishes the need to have many children for support in later life.

The youthful part of a population requires different efforts. Young people represent the future of a society, a renewal of ways of thinking as well as modes of production; but they can fulfill this dream only if the necessary resources are made available for their education. The burden is, of course, that much greater since the largest proportion of young people is to be found in the poorest countries and the field of education is one where external aid generally makes only the slightest difference. What scope can there be, after all, to educational and technical assistance programs?—to the sending of a few teachers to help train local ones? This is not to say that other forms of aid cannot make complementary, though essential contributions, in this field. However, the emphasis must be on areas where the effort can be most effective—in other words, to guarantee a minimum of subsistence in those countries menaced by famine, to finance infrastructure, to promote conditions to attract investment can be invaluable, if done on a sufficient scale. It would allow the internal resources of the country in question to be devoted to the support and training of its youth.

The evident conclusion of all this is that no developing country can afford to do without long-term plans concerning its population's evolution. It cannot ignore the fluctuations in the fertility rate and the effects thereof, combined with increased life expectancy, on the profile of the working population or on the investment in education required by an ever-increasing number of young people. All efforts will be doomed to failure if these factors are not taken into account. The task that is called for is one where technical assistance and, in particular, the aid of international organizations is most necessary. The world may yet avoid catastrophe in passing through the present demographic transition, but this depends on our being able to combine our view of the needs of those growing populations with the analyses done by each of the developing nations. Otherwise the population explosion may destroy the stimuli that are the mainsprings of development.

4

The World Bank president Robert McNamara has presented us with two striking aspects of the developing world: the growing gap between countries and also the gaps within each country.

First, let us consider his speech at the UNCTAD conference in Santiago.* The first decade of development (1960-70) as defined by the United Nations foresaw an average rate of growth of 5 percent in the Third World. While this general objective has been reached, it has only been through gaps so wide as to accentuate the inequalities.

The oil exporting countries which represent less than 4 percent of the Third World's population and a revenue much higher than the average, grew by 8.4 percent per year. One can imagine how big a further leap forward must have occurred since the quadrupling of oil prices.

In the countries which already had a GNP of $500 per capita, and 9 percent of the population, GNP grew at a rate of 6.2 percent. The countries between $200 and $500, with 20 percent of the population, had a growth rate of 5.4 percent. Below $200 per capita, we find 67 percent of the population and a mere 3.9 percent growth rate.

However, these figures have only little significance, since they confuse population and production. Incomes per head are more meaningful. These same poorest countries raise their per capita income by only 1.5 percent per year; it rises to 2.4 percent for the category of countries immediately

---

*Incorporated in Chapter 4 of Robert S. McNamara, *One Hundred Countries, Two Billion People: The Dimensions of Development*. (New York: Praeger, 1973).

above; to 4.2 percent for the countries with more than $500 per capita, and to 5.2 percent for the oil exporters.

INEQUALITIES AMONG AND WITHIN COUNTRIES

Whether one looks at the initial situation, or whether one projects trends, in the industrialized world as in the underdeveloped world, the picture of growing inequality everywhere in the world is frightening. One can question figures such as $50 per capita per annum; it only highlights the limitations of national accounting systems which do not take into account services that individuals or families render themselves. The figures fail to express the profound differences in prices from country to country. Between the richest and the poorest countries, the spread in per capita income is supposed to be from 50 to 5,000, that is to say from 1 to 100. Even if the lowest figure were doubled and the highest one lowered to take into account the very high prices paid for services in the most advanced countries, there would still be a spread from 1 to 40 between the two extremes. If the GNP at one end of the scale doesn't go up by more than 1.5 percent per year while it rises by 3.5 percent or 5 percent at the other, there can be no limit to the width of the gap. Still, it is evident that the present growth rate in the richest countries cannot be extrapolated indefinitely. It is, in fact, not so much the gap that counts, it is rather that the situation in the poorest countries seems to be almost entirely without solution. All the indications point in the same direction: low literacy rates (scarcely 5 percent in some countries) as well as energy per capita, and even cars, telephones, newspapers all being at infinitesimal levels. The most monstrous aspect of it all is, however, the low life expectancy. The spread is from 75 years for women and 70 years for men in the fully developed countries to less than 40 years on the average for the Third World. Here, in the strong words of Mr. McNamara, the greatest part of the population of the world is deprived of more than a third of the lifespan to which it should be able to aspire. Even so, this desperately low average conceals even graver, more drastic situations: rates of 34 to 41 years for most of the African countries. If one needed an absolute indicator of misery, surely this is it. Given the incidence of infant mortality, it expresses the malnutrition, the lack of hygiene and medical care that beset so much of the world.

And yet, this picture of inequalities between countries does not reveal the full extent of the tragedy. To it must be added the inequalities that exist within each country. This was one of the themes taken up by McNamara before a World Bank assembly in Nairobi. Official statistics in this field are hopelessly inadequate, in the developing world as well as in the industrialized world. The World Bank and some private institutions have tried to shed some light on the matter. According to McNamara, there are 40 developing countries for which statistics are available. Typically, 20 percent of the population in these countries absorbed 50 percent of the national income, while on the other hand, the poorest 20 percent received only 5 percent of the total. This works out to the highest segment taking 2.75 times the average national income and the lowest only one-quarter. An 11 to 1 spread such as this reaches even more incredible proportions if one compares the extremes at each end of the scale, the richest 2 percent or 5 percent, for example, compared with the poorest 5 percent. Yet it is at this lowest level that attention must be focused; it is here that 800 million people each account for $100 per year, less than $.30 per day!

Thus we see that average figures are deceptive, and all the more so when they refer to growth rates. For they seem invariably higher for the Third World as a whole since those who lead the pack develop faster: the average is affected upward by their share in the total. The same holds true within each country: per capita income seems to grow faster as the privileged few, already so far ahead, see their share grow and add to the whole. What is more important, therefore, is to know just how the poorest elements in each society are fed, clothed, cared for, and housed. This kind of comparison, for which so little data is available, would upset many accepted ideas even as regards relations between certain developing countries and certain industrialized ones. It would also raise many questions about the significance of aid and the strategy of development.

FINANCIAL FLOWS

The debate on contributions to developing countries always seems to swing between two poles: on the one hand, one tots up financial flow (including private company investments), the difference between the loans and repayments and even the amounts of credit from foreign suppliers; on the other, one counts only gifts or loans with favorable conditions, that is to say whose rates of interest, repayment terms, and extensions are much more generous than those of the ordinary financial market. This question has in fact been clarified some time ago; loans at market rates cannot be assimilated to aid, and credits from suppliers are not much more than assistance to the producers and exporters of the country which gives the credit, rather than to the country which receives it. In fact, many of the balance-of-payments problems experienced by developing countries can be attributed to much credit granted at terms which are too short to allow internal investment to generate sufficient production through which to repay. It has also often been underlined that there are distinct disadvantages to the practice of tying aid to obligations to purchase in the aid-giving country or to use its carriers for transporting merchandise. Whatever the external deficits may be by which certain industrialized countries justify aid with strings attached, it is clear that it would be unnecessary to impose such obligations except insofar as the benefiting countries would not otherwise spontaneously buy from the donor countries or use their transportation. This is tantamount to saying that in such cases their prices or the cost of their transportation are higher than those of their competitors. Aid expressed in money, for example in dollars, should therefore be adjusted downwards so as to reflect the actual contribution and make allowances for excessive prices of supplies and transportation.

There are two reasons for raising these questions at this time. The first is that as soon as a country goes from having a deficit to having a balance or a surplus, all possible justification for tying its aid disappears; the aid should immediately lose all strings. The second reason is that we are witnessing circumstances where traditional surplus countries are suffering from large deficits due to the price rises in their imports of energy; they are thus inclined to reconsider any aid they may be giving. It is revealing in this respect to look at what part of their sales of equipment normally went to developing countries. Some Third World countries will, of course, manage to raise their incomes thanks to the increase in oil prices and in the price of certain raw materials. For the others, however, this may mean a combination of higher purchase costs, stagnant or lowered receipts and, if attention is not paid in time, a decline in the amount of aid received from outside. The industrialized countries will ignore at their own peril the needs created by the present situation. A reduction in aid could condemn their production structures to even more painful adjustments than those resulting from the price rises of many of their imported supplies. It would be the worst possible time to add to the slowdown which affects, among others, the automobile industry, a further slowdown in heavy industry. In periods of full employment or even over-employment, foreign aid may well seem to be a sacrifice—however marginal—or a claim made on resources to the detriment of domestic needs. In the face of the uncertainties which threaten employment in the industrialized world, these countries will in fact be helping themselves by keeping up their foreign aid—even if they have to borrow from the oil producers to maintain or even increase their aid to those countries which lack resources. While there has been nothing more deceptive than the inclusion of export credits in foreign aid figures, we have now reached the stage where aid can be of just as much help to producers in industrialized countries as exports credits.

Incentives of this kind are not useless. On the whole, the aid picture to date, even including the sum total of capital transfers to developing countries, offers a sad spectacle. The share of their resources which the advanced countries have devoted to foreign aid gets smaller all the time. There are only two or three countries which, having started off in a very small way, have increased their percentage. For all others it has declined. France, which used to be in the lead with transfers amounting to 2.1 percent of its GNP in 1961, fell to 1 percent in 1971 and to 0.67 percent in terms of genuine aid (as against 1.35 percent ten years earlier). The United States has dropped to thirteenth place among fourteen donors in percentage of income assigned to aid. A Development Aid Committee (DAC) was formed within the OECD with the object of encouraging industrialized countries to urge one another along. The supreme irony of the situation is that the creation of this committee was an American initiative and that it has been presided over by one American after another.

The United Nations conceived the idea of ten-year development programs. For the second decade (1965-75) the industrialized countries beat their breasts and recognized the insufficiency of their contributions; they subscribed without hesitation to the idea of progressively raising the percentage of their resources to be devoted to development; they swore to reach 1 percent by 1975, and 0.7 percent aid factor. As things stand now, one cannot but sing a different tune. Lowering his sights somewhat, McNamara has asked that these objectives be met over a longer period; having failed to reach them in 1975, the industrialized countries should set 1980 as the new target year. In the prospects for growth, as they were before the energy crisis, he noted that a slightly higher percentage for development, based on a rapidly increasing revenue, would still leave the richest countries with 98 percent of their surplus resources to devote to domestic needs and demands, internal consumption, a search for greater equality, public services, defense, investments.

Let us come right out and say it: these puny percentages—1 percent, 0.7 percent—make no sense at all. There is not a single country in which taxation is strictly applied, let alone those countries in which income taxes bring in no more than one-third of that which is provided for by the letter of the law. Everywhere there is a margin between private incomes as computed in the national accounts and by the taxation authorities. Everywhere there are perfectly legal loopholes which most often benefit the highest incomes. It would be difficult to argue that taxation could not be tightened in order to glean another 2 percent or 3 percent of national income, without, in fact, taking anything away from the poorer classes of citizens. These 1 percent contributions or 0.7 percent aid objectives have nothing more than historical significance. They are approximately the order of magnitude of the U.S. effort in the 1950s. The real limits were imposed by the fact that the external balance of the United States represents only 4 percent or 5 percent of its GNP: such is the value of all imports and exports of a country that essentially supplies its own market. With such a relatively minimal foreign trade sector, it was difficult to set aside a surplus which would be much more than a quarter or a fifth of external receipts. When its very profitable investments outside the country began to reach this figure, America found itself with a deficit. While today it is showing its ability to regain lost ground, paradoxically enough, an entirely new situation could result from a growing U.S. dependence on imports of raw materials and energy. If the United States is forced to devote $35 or $50 billion more in this area alone, its economic structure will come to resemble more closely those found in other industrialized countries, where external transactions take up a much larger part of the total economic activity. Hence, far from constituting an obstacle, this restructuring could remove a stumbling block.

Chaotic Aid

But the sums involved are not the only questions to be tackled. In spite of the efforts of the DAC, there has been so little of a conceptual framework and so little coordinating among donor countries, that it is impossible to discern the slightest rhyme or reason to the way in which funds have been distributed among countries.

One might have supposed that aid, whether free or in the form of "soft" loans, would go first to the poorest countries. In fact, the simplest statistical investigation would show the most unbelievable disorder. Unfortunately, the figures are not all known. Even though UNCTAD, which, contrary to the General Agreement on Tariffs and Trade (GATT), was to deal with the Third World and with East-West relations, the statistics it gathered do not include even one figure for transfers from the East.

Interestingly enough, one must go to OECD sources to get a general view of aid and loans supplied by the Soviet Union, other Eastern European countries, and China. The information is made up of fragmentary indications supplied by the donors themselves, and more largely by estimates made by the American State Department. It is, in a sense, quite remarkable that the Chinese republic should have begun offering aid to other countries so early in its history, when the Chinese themselves had such a low income. The Soviet approach has been to make loans over

KEY TO FIGURES

Country	Number	Country	Number	Country	Number	Country	Number
Afghanistan	1	Gambia	37	Malaysia	73	Singapore	107
Algeria	2	Ghana	38	Maldives	74	Solomon	108
Angola	3	Gibraltar	39	Mali	75	Somalia	109
Dutch Antilles	4	Gilbert	40	Malta	76	Spain	110
Argentina	5	Greece	41	Martinique	77	Sri Lanka	111
Bahamas	6	Guadelupe	42	Mauritania	78	St. Helena	112
Bahrain	7	Guatemala	43	Maurice	79	St. Pierre	
Barbados	8	Guinea	44	Mexico	80	Miquelon	113
Bermuda	9	Equatorial Guinea	45	Morocco	81	Sudan	114
Bhutan	10	Portuguese Guinea	46	Mozambique	82	Surinam	115
Bolivia	11	French Guyana	47	Nepal	83	Swaziland	116
Botswana	12	Haiti	48	New Caledonia	84	Syria	117
Brazil	13	Honduras	49	New Hebrides	85	Taiwan	118
Brunei	14	Guyana	50	Nicaragua	86	Tanzania	119
Burma	15	British Honduras	51	Niger	87	Afars and Issas	120
Burundi	16	Hong Kong	52	Nigeria	88	Thailand	121
Cameroun	17	India	53	Oman	89	Timor	122
Cape Verde	18	Indonesia	54	Easter Island	90	Togo	123
Central African		Iran	55	Pakistan*	91	Tonga	124
Republic	19	Iraq	56	Panama	92	Trinidad	125
Chad	20	Israel	57	Papuasia N.G.	93	Tunisia	126
Chile	21	Ivory Coast	58	Paraguay	94	Turkey	127
Colombia	22	Jamaica	59	Peru	95	Uganda	128
Comoro	23	Jordan	60	Philippines	96	Arab Emirates	129
Congo	24	Kenya	61	French Polynesia	97	Upper Volta	130
Costa Rica	25	Khmer Republic	62	Qatar	98	Uruguay	131
Cuba	26	South Korea	63	Reunion	99	Venezuela	132
Cyprus	27	Kuwait	64	Rhodesia	100	South Vietnam	133
Dahomey	28	Laos	65	Rwanda	101	Wallis-Futuna	134
Dominican Republic	29	Lebanon	66	Soa Tome and		Caribbeans	135
Ecuador	30	Lesotho	67	Principe	102	Samoa	136
Egypt	31	Liberia	68	Saudi Arabia	103	North Yemen	137
Salvador	32	Libya	69	Senegal	104	Yemen Republic	138
Ethiopia	33	Macao	70	Seychelles	105	Yugoslavia	139
Falkland	34	Madagascar	71	Sierra Leone	106	Zaire	140
Fiji	35	Malawi	72			Zambia	141
Gabon	36			*Bangladesh included			

FIGURE 1

Income per Head and Share of Nonagricultural Population

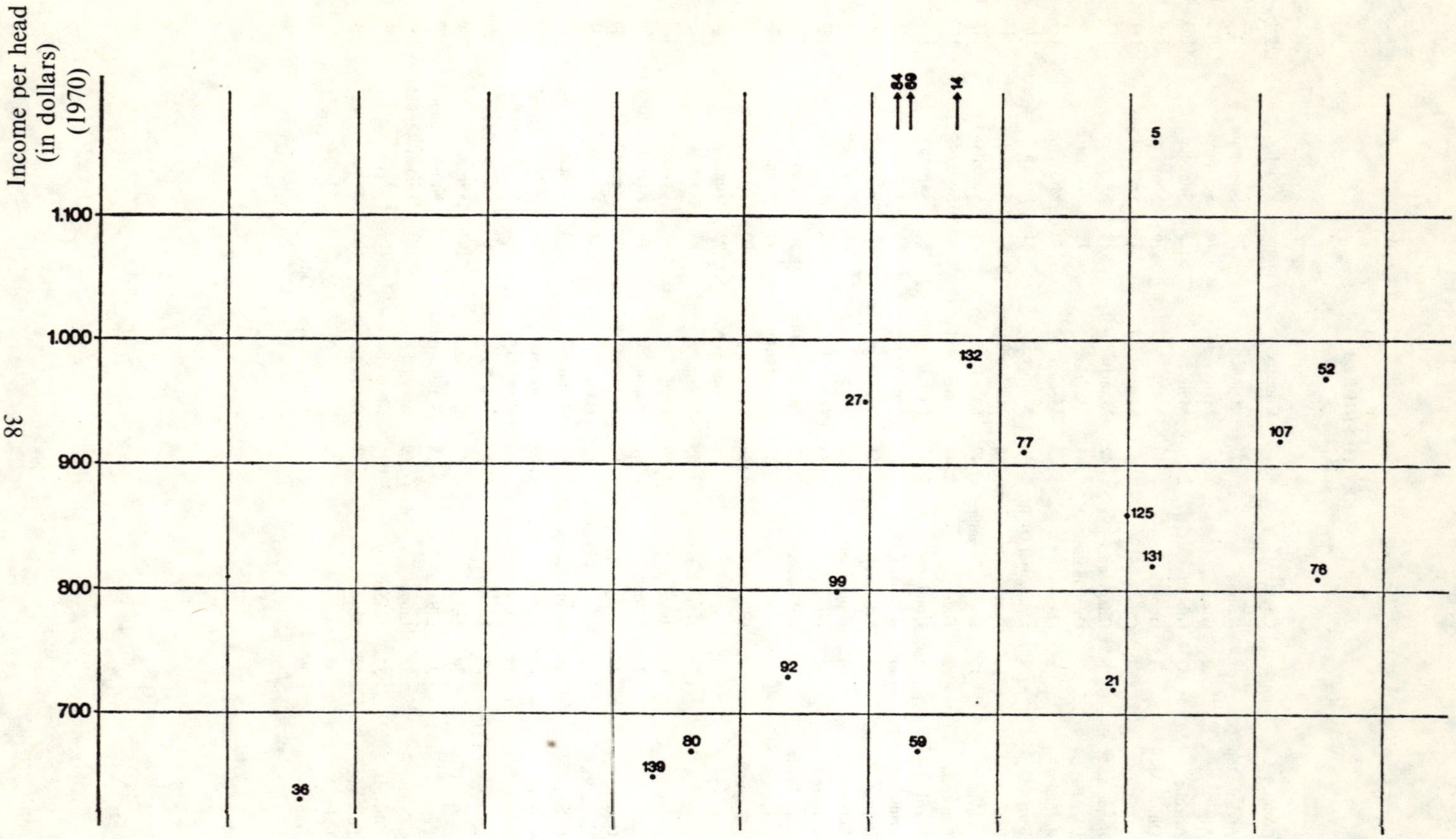

Income per head
(in dollars)
(1970)

1.100
1.000
900
800
700

5•

74
88
79

132•

27•

77•

52•

107•

125•
131•

21•

76•

99•

92•

50•

80•
139•

36•

38

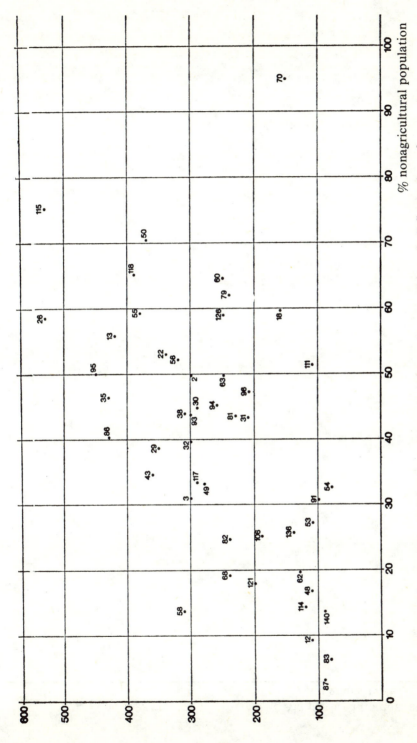

% nonagricultural population

Note: See key to figures for countries that correspond to numbers on this and all figures hereafter.

39

FIGURE 2

Aid in Relation to Income per Head in Benefiting Countries

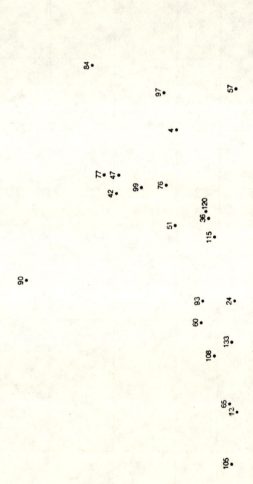

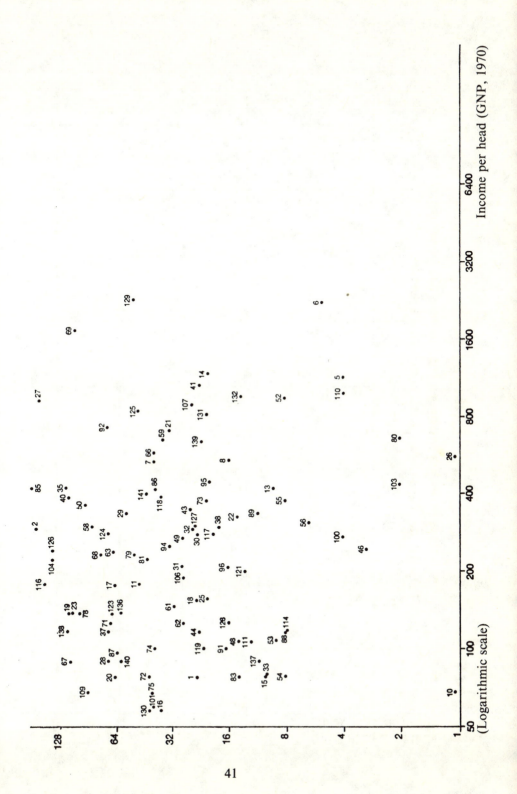

(Logarithmic scale)

Income per head (GNP, 1970)

41

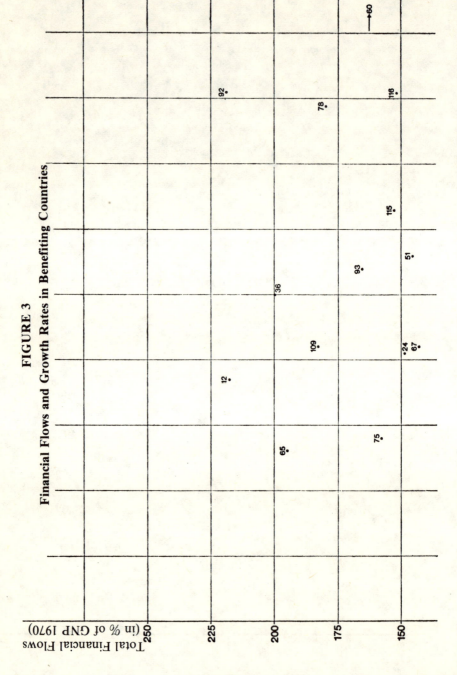

FIGURE 3

Financial Flows and Growth Rates in Benefiting Countries

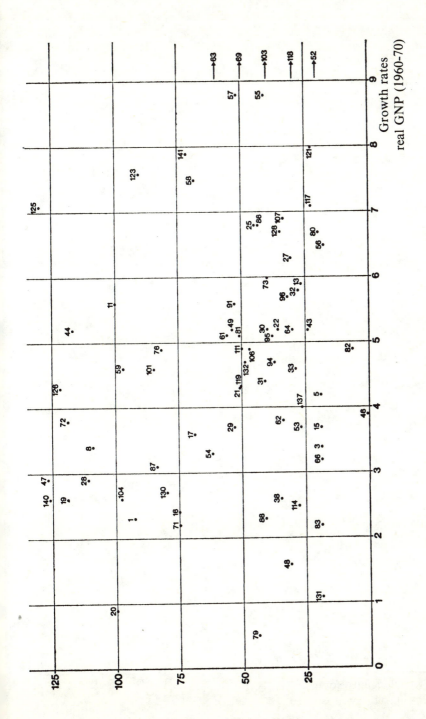

Growth rates
real GNP (1960-70)

FIGURE 4

Direct Investment in Relation to Income per Head

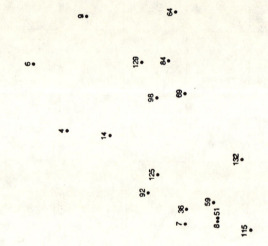

Direct investment per head (in dollars book value, end 1971)

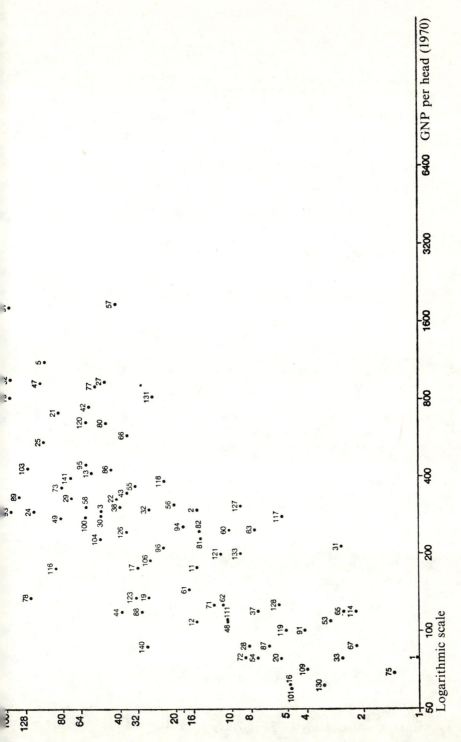

GNP per head (1970)

Logarithmic scale

FIGURE 5

Direct Investment in Relation to Growth Rate

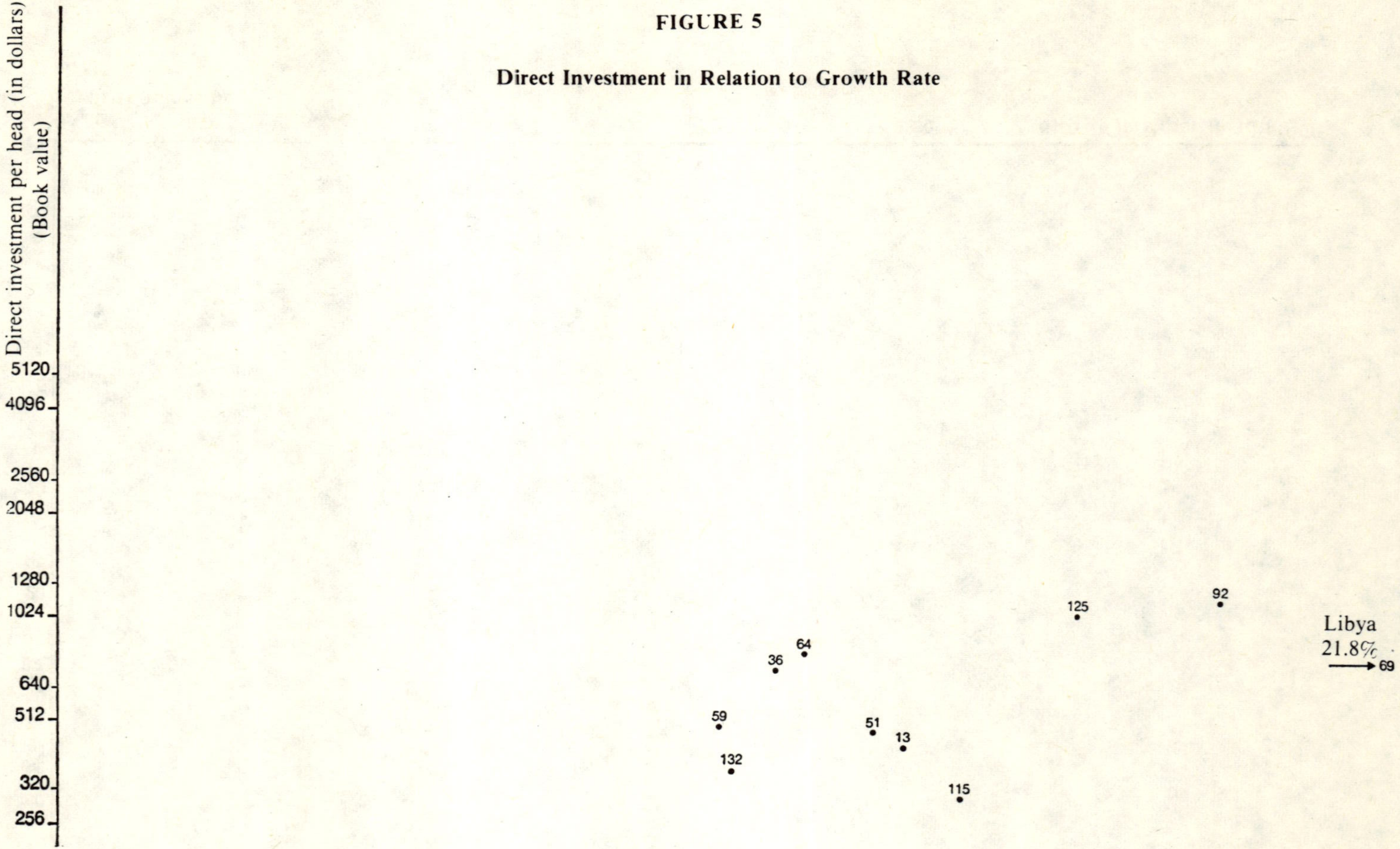

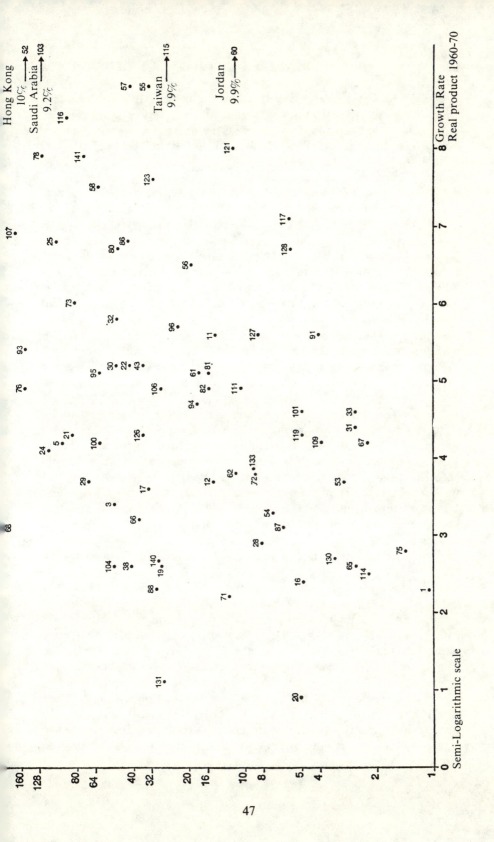

Semi-Logarithmic scale

Growth Rate
Real product 1960-70

Hong Kong
10% ⟶ 52
Saudi Arabia
9.2% ⟶ 103

Taiwan
9.9% ⟶ 115

Jordan
9.9% ⟶ 60

47

twelve years at 2.5 percent. The total furnished by the Communist countries over twenty years, and at least half of which has gone to developing countries of the Communist world, is on the order of $15 billion. This is approximately what the Western world transfers in one year; scarcely enough to redress the balance so utterly disturbed by the Western countries' practices.

As far as the distribution of Western aid goes, there is a very simple test one can apply. One can add up the accrued total per receiving country between 1960 and 1970. One can also reckon the level of incomes in each country, in 1970, for example. By dividing one and then the other figure by the population it is as easy to obtain the amount of aid per capita as the amount of income per capita. Let us transfer all these countries onto a diagram (See Figure 1) where the per capita incomes follow the abscissas and the per capita aid the ordinates.* If the higher aid contributions had gone to the poorer countries, then there would be a cluster of points in the upper left-hand corner of the diagram; that is, low income, high aid. But that corner is empty. In fact the countries are spread out in a nebulous pattern—similar amounts per capita go to countries in very different situations; in some cases the highest amount of aid per capita goes to countries whose per capita incomes are among the highest.

In fact another method of distribution is possible: financial assistance would go to the most promising places. The aid dispensers have always wavered between adopting the criterion of elementary needs and that of absorption capacity for internal development. Here again, one can cross-check; this time not only taking amounts of aid as a factor but also net financial flows including direct investments and surplus of loans and credits on repayment. The statistics reveal clearly what this flow represents for each receiving country in proportion to its GNP. Ten years of financial contributions can represent as little as a few percent of the income of 1970 alone; or in certain cases, an amount equivalent to or even

----

*International publications provide figures on a comparable basis with a considerable delay. It is thus that the attempts of the United Nations to estimate the effects of the oil and other raw materials' price rise on the balances of different developing countries are based on hypothetical adjustments to the 1970 exchanges. In this diagram, as in others, the use of slightly outdated figures does not have very serious consequences. The structure of the active population changes very slowly; the relative position of a country with regard to per capita income or growth rate does not change very suddenly. The validity of the correlations, or their lack, remains the same.

double that. At least, one should be entitled to expect a connection between this proportion of outside contributions in relation to income, on the one hand, and the varying rates of growth of the countries in question, on the other. In this same way the average rate of investments over a certain period, as a percentage of GNP, can be related to the rate of growth of this GNP; the relation thus defines what is called the marginal capital/output ratio. In other words, and by analogy, what is sought is a marginal coefficient of outside capital as it applies to the developing countries. Once again, one must come down a few pegs. If financial assistance had proved efficient, the cloud of dots on the graph (See Figure 3) which relates its proportion to the GNP and the rate of GNP growth in the receiving countries, would be found close to the diagonal. In fact, most of them are to be found near the axis of the abscissas. The influx of capital compared to the GNP is generally low and there is no relation to the rate of growth. This does not preclude, of course, that in a particular country growth accelerates when capital flows increase. What is at stake here is the allocation among countries. There, one can see a line emerging where the relationship between influx and the rate of growth appears to be complementary. This is the case of a small number of countries, generally quite small themselves. In other words, it is not too expensive to help countries with small populations, in which case the contributions are relatively large enough to be effective.

Thus, these simple analyses lead to the most depressing kind of conclusion, for they demonstrate that aid has not gone to where it is most urgently needed, that the totals of capital flows have not been related to capacity for development and that they have not, as a rule, favored development.

A few figures will summarize this total absence of planning, show this unbelievable anarchy. In the period 1960 to 1970, the poorest countries,—those with less than $100 per capita,—accounted for 14.1 percent of the population of the Third World. They received 11.2 percent of the aid. Between $100 and $200 per capita are to be found 46 percent of the population and 26 percent of the aid; between $200 and $300, 12 percent of the population and 24 percent of the aid; between $300 and $400, 9.5 percent of the population and 14.8 percent of the aid. In other words, the poorest countries receive a share of the aid which is far lower than their part of the population as a whole. Where the level of income is higher, the distribution of aid is more generous. One has to go beyond revenues of $400 per capita before the share of aid again becomes inferior to the share of the population; in the $400 to $600 bracket the proportions are 4 percent and 7.4 percent respectively.

The reasons for this senseless distribution become even clearer as one examines some of the cases at the extremities of the graphs. A large share of the total aid has been absorbed by a few individual countries and by a few bilateral aid programs.

In some cases, per capita aid, if taken over a ten-year period, comes close to equaling the per capita income for 1970. It is even higher for Guadeloupe, Martinique, and South Vietnam, twice as much for Laos; for French Guyana it equals the 1970 income; in Reunion and Chad it is three-quarters; in Senegal, the Democratic Republic of the Congo, and the Central African Republic, two-thirds; in Algeria, New Caledonia, and Surinam, one-half. The picture is quite clear: France and the Netherlands have been taking care of their overseas departments and their former colonies, and the United States has been trying to keep two Asian countries within its orbit. As for India or Indonesia, in ten years the amount of aid per capita has not amounted to 10 percent of the per capita income of the final year. By oversimplifying only a little, one cannot but conclude that the percentage is tragically inadequate in most of the developing countries. The poor countries don't manage to attract 1 percent of their income in external aid.

The aid of the Eastern bloc countries is also very narrowly oriented. The Soviet Union's aid to the non-Communist world is growing somewhat. The actual transfers remain much smaller than those made to the Communist world and consist mostly of low-interest loans. The totals up to 1973 amount to $2.7 billion for the non-Communist world and $8.7 billion for the Communist countries. A large part of this sum went to Cuba and North Vietnam. In the non-Communist world, this economic aid is accompanied by military aid. The principal beneficiaries are, on the one hand, Egypt, Syria, and Iraq, as was seen in their conflict with Israel; and, on the other hand, India, as was seen in its conflict with Pakistan. China has, from 1953 to 1971, signed aid agreements for over $4.6 billion. These agreements have fluctuated and diminished appreciably at the time of the cultural revolution, and North Vietnam and Cuba also received a large share. Among the non-Communist countries, Pakistan received aid for similar and contrary reasons that the USSR gave aid to India. It is interesting to note the differences in orientation here. The Soviet Union finances heavy industry which reflects what has been its own type of development. China is the only country that has concentrated on small-scale farming and has sent its experts to live in and share the conditions of the local populations. It wasn't until the building of the Tanzania-Zambia railway link that China undertook to contribute to a vast infrastructure program for which it furnished not only materials and techniques, but also labor.

The efforts of the Eastern and Western blocs thus have many similarities. There is no way of rectifying so meager, so inequitable, so inefficient, and politically so dangerous a pattern of aid allocation; it cries out for a radical revision. There is no lack of organizations concerned with development; soon there will be too many. Most of the research done by the United Nations concentrates on development. The United Nations manages two or three funds, one which does preliminary studies for investments and another which studies population problems. All of UNCTAD, with its periodic conferences, focuses on the general problem of development. The OECD, with the DAC at its side, looks at the situation from the donors' point of view. Excellent studies have been done at the Center for Development, also created by the OECD. Except at the World Bank, which looks at these questions from its own angle, no general design of any sort seems to have emerged. While the World Bank group has managed to increase very rapidly the financing which it grants at ordinary or preferential rates, doubling it in a period of five years, over the past few years these transactions have represented only 10 percent of total transfers. The bank's president has underlined the need for concentrating on the poorest countries and segments of populations. To meet this need he has called for an increase in the proportion of agricultural development programs. But 20 percent of the World Bank's effort in this area still represents only 2 percent of the total.

THE PRIORITIES

There is thus a dire need for a conceptual framework. What are the first priorities to which all aid programs must be geared? Who should give the aid? How and according to what principles should it be distributed? These are the basic conditions to be defined. They are the only way to keep the Third World countries from having to compete with each other to curry favor with the aid-giving countries.

What are the aims? Much has been made of the growing gap, and the risks of widening it even further, between the industrialized countries and the Third World. But to put the problems in these terms is to accept from the start that there can be no solution. Unless absolute shortages put an end to the continuing progress of the rich countries, or unless they choose to turn towards an entirely different form of civilization, the fact remains that the higher a community's income, the easier it should be for it to set aside some savings—which is another way of saying that the higher the income, the faster it grows. What can and should be done is quite another matter: to concentrate first of all on the most wretched and seemingly hopeless situations. From this point of view, 1 percent of the GNP of the richest countries begins to make more sense: by the 1980s this would mean $30 billion per year. If there are, as the World Bank's statistics show, 800 million people in the poorest countries and in the poor regions of the advanced countries, who have only $100 per year, these $30 billion would allow for an immediate 30 percent increase in their incomes. This could make the difference between hunger, sickness, absence of hygiene, and a minimum which would permit survival. At least this cruelest of inequities, this enormous difference in life expectancy between the modern and backward countries, would be reduced. But at the same time another obstacle looms; however great this need, any effort in this direction will also serve to speed up the formidable growth of the world's population, without at the same time developing the resources to clothe, feed, house, and provide medical care for these innumerable masses.

A second effort is thus equally indispensable. Subsistence aid must therefore go together with assistance to development in the proper sense of the term. The system cannot rely only on donations. Criteria must be established to classify contributions according to whether they are to be in the form of free gifts, long-term, low-interest loans; or whether they can be assured by international investments, possibly subject to certain conditions or matched with complementary financing.

If emphasis is, indeed, to be placed on the fight against the direst poverty, it will be found to be in the countries with the largest agricultural populations. However wretched the urban proletariat in these countries may be, the most profound poverty will be found in the countryside. Even if our figures for per capita income and the breakdown of the working population between agriculture and the rest are not always for the same year, the connection is so obvious that this statistical imperfection has no bearing on the results. On a diagram showing the percentage of non-agricultural population on the abscissa and the per capita income on the ordinate, the developing countries will be found along the diagonal; at the lowest level are the countries which have almost no population employed in other than agriculture, whereas at the highest are those whose agricultural population represents only a small fraction of the whole. It is also a fact that the greater the number employed on the land, the smaller the productivity. Hence another vicious circle: peasants so poor that they have no means to buy seed, fertilizer, or even rudimentary tools which would help them to raise the profitability of their land or their labor. It is all very well to create dams which allow dry land to be irrigated, to invent new strains of seed which permit miraculous increases in crops. Only the most well-off farmers can afford the installations which will bring the new water to their fields, or the price of these new hybrids of wheat or rice. In the end all this will only serve to increase the inequities, and to chase from their land those small farmers who have not the means to expand because lower prices and high interest rates have ruined them and the market now supplied by modern production no longer needs them. The only way out is with a large transfer of funds from the rich countries, for neither the peasants nor the governments of the poorest countries have the means of paying for the public works, the seeds and the fertilizers. To bring this about requires a revolution in the attitudes and motives of the donor countries. It is, of course, more spectacular to build great dams or factories, more grandiose to appear at inauguration ceremonies than to subsidize obscure but vital things like minor agricultural hydraulics, the creation of advisory services, or to make gifts, in kind or money, of seeds and fertilizer.

Food, medical supplies, the basic means of increasing the yield in the mass of small farms—all this must be given thorough concerted effort. Beyond these are the tasks which call upon the public means of the developing countries' own governments. There the tax resources may be insufficient, not only because tax collection may be inefficient, but simply because production and income are too low. Thus, an immediate effort for improvement of education, housing, and medical care is called for. There is no question but that this would contribute to improving productivity by means of better qualified labor, and a reduction of disease or physiological weakness. These results are, unfortunately, indirect and so uncertain that it is hard to depend on them for the repayment of foreign loans. This is surely an area where money, if it is not given outright, must be advanced over a long period and at very low interest rates.

A REGIONAL POLICY FOR THE WORLD

Aid to development must come to be governed by an entirely different kind of logic. In the nineteenth century, it was thought that the fewer the investments that had been made in a region, the more profitable any new investment would be. In this way the free flow of capital would tend to fill the gaps. However, it is now well known that for this reasoning to be valid, certain basic conditions have to be fulfilled. A region without the necessary infrastructure cannot attract productive investments; it needs a means of transportation, a supply of energy, preferably also a link to ports, and even the means of assuring the health and training of its labor. The first companies to arrive on the spot are, moreover, disadvantaged by not having their customers and suppliers right on hand. In other words, they do not enjoy the external economies which accumulate as more and more firms install themselves and each new firm benefits from the facilities which depend as much on public investment as on the network of already established firms and on the gradual emerging of a trained labor force. It is in this sense that the industrialized countries are in fact carrying out a kind of regional economic development policy, though not always in a consistent manner. When public authorities finance basic infrastructure, offer subsidies or tax reductions, sometimes grants of land for the construction of plants in backward or declining areas, it is no longer considered that they thus distort competition. On the contrary, such measures compensate for an initial disadvantage and, if they are correctly calculated and administered, they should be gradually eliminated as they meet with success. Such facilities can in this way make the old assumption come true and make it more profitable for firms to install themselves in hitherto unexploited areas.

The growth of international trade and the development of multinational firms make it all the more necessary to think of development programs in terms of regional development policies on a worldwide scale. Once per capita income in a growing number of countries rises above the levels of poverty requiring grant aid, one can start to rely more on investment flows for development. Certain conditions for such investment must, of course, be assured, that is, an adequate framework which will allow initial disadvantages to be overcome. In many cases the firms themselves can be called upon to participate in the financing of such infrastructure—the housing or the education facilities which are essential complements to the firms' establishment and operation. There are also many cases in which separate sources of financing are necessary. Since the aim is to facilitate investments which will eventually be profitable, intergovernmental loans as well as those from the World Bank or regional development banks may in such cases sometimes approximate market conditions and even follow a borrowing-to-lend pattern.

The foregoing assumes, of course, that in each country the total of resources obtained on a repayable basis remains within limits and is spread over periods in which the country's income from the sale of goods and services or, where necessary, through new inflows of capital, will allow it to meet its obligations. The fact that there is no centralized means of identifying the risks assumed by many developing countries has led to the hasty creation of a number of consortiums which have no choice but to accept a staggering of debt payments or to relend money which would normally go to repay creditors or even to cancel some of the loans. The result is that aid is granted after the fact, without having been deliberate or planned, as the mere consequence of an unthought-out lending policy. To take this kind of way out only serves to blur the picture, to undo even further whatever coherence there may be in aid grants. It underlines the need for the criteria and framework (both for subsistence aid and development aid) being defined in advance and through common consent.

Channels and Criteria

Through this sort of approach, the bilateral or multilateral nature of financial cooperation would lose its importance. Undoubtedly, its being channeled through international institutions has the advantage of avoiding any apparent relationships of dependence. Once objectives and principles are fixed in common from the outset, this aspect is much reduced. As was recognized in the U.S.-sponsored Peterson Report, another advantage of the multilateral context is that it eliminates much of the duplication of studies done by various donors and prospective lenders. However, there are cases where one country is better placed than another to offer assistance to a particular country by virtue of a long relationship or a better mutual understanding. It can be said for the international financial institutions, whether they be the World Bank or regional banks, that in their examination of projects and in their decision-making, they *do* bring together developed and underdeveloped countries. However, as has been clearly shown, for example by the Inter-American Development Bank, these institutions can only borrow against capital furnished by a highly industrialized country, the United States in this case, which, in effect, has a determining influence, and exercises a kind of unofficial veto on how resources are used. One of the drawbacks to these institutions is that their industrialized members are all Western countries. If aid questions are to be brought out of the anarchy in which they are to be found today, there will have to be some coordination between East and West. Instead of treating the developing world as if it were a stake in a political game, East and West should consider the extent of its misery and the immensity of its needs as providing an exceptional opportunity for a joint effort.

One of the most desirable forms of assistance would be one in which funds and manpower do not necessarily come from the same place. Countries which are themselves just emerging from underdevelopment are often able to provide experts who are more aware of local problems, better able to identify situations which demand urgent remedies, and more able to adjust simple techniques to particular circumstances. France has given some examples of technical aid which it has financed, but which it put into effect by employing, in one instance, Tunisians. Generally speaking, the unequal stages of development of different countries should make it possible to make use of the more advanced among the less advanced to show the way to others, to act as a sort of reservoir of the kind of expertise which is most appropriate.

As for the ways and means of external public contributions, it has long been debated whether they should bear on specific projects (as implied by the statutes of the World Bank), or be more widely based, in terms of general programs. This second approach was the one adopted by the Alliance for Progress. The Charter of Punta del Este, launching the alliance, required that each country establish a plan for reaching certain accepted growth objectives, improvement in housing and education, tax reform, reductions of balance-of-payments deficits, etc.

It is only normal to expect each developed country, as much as each underdeveloped country, to discuss its policies with its partners, for the former inevitably affect the latter. Even the United States or Britain cannot avoid this obligation when they require outside financial cooperation. It is even surprising, in a world where capital moves about so freely, that any country should still be free to fix its own interest rates and thereby provoke massive movements of speculation. The principle by which it is left up to each country to reestablish its own balance of payments, instead of a country consulting with its partners on what mutually complementary actions might be taken, is yet another example of how *not* to strive for the most efficient means of recovery and how *not* to avoid the kinds of measures which serve only to create further difficulty.

Nonetheless, the fact is that external financing of general programs implies a direct interference in the case of developing countries. In order to eliminate this discrimination and the relationship of dependence, it would be best to go back to the idea of financing specific projects—provided, of course, that they are defined in an efficient and consistent way. The World Bank has accepted the idea that the foreign currency expenditure financing to which its statutes now limit it, should be extended not only to direct costs for equipment or imported assistance, but also to derived imports resulting from the sudden growth of revenue and demand stimulated by the investments themselves. The European Bank has in certain cases sought to contribute to the development of particularly backward regions through financing interrelated projects which provide mutual benefits. However, one cannot avoid certain obligations of a general nature on rates of development or on the conditions for keeping economies in balance, but they should serve simply as a background against which projects can be appraised—in the same way that a banker considers the general situation and future of a firm along with the particular investment for which his aid is being solicited.

The clear distinction between two types of external aid, subsistence aid and development aid, must be reflected in the negotiation methods which are used. Aid, whose purposes are to provide food, medical supplies, and the means of raising the yields of small farms, should be tied to no conditions at all, once its objectives and material context have been clearly defined. Assistance to development, on the other hand, calls for an entirely different approach. Its role is as an indispensable complement for productive investment; it should be considered as a regional development policy on a worldwide scale. To be consistent, development aid would be applied in the context of regions and not of particular countries—whether it be a disadvantaged area like northeastern Brazil, or Bengal, or, on the other hand, a group of small countries such as those of Central America. By this means one might escape the dilemma which results from the link between offering assistance to a country and negotiating with its government: that is, the problem of whether to support an indefensible government or, by condemning it, to abandon the country to its mercies. The representatives of donor countries or international institutions would, of course, find their place in the regional development banks which already exist or which must be created; there would be one, for instance, for northeastern Brazil, another for Central America.

This kind of change is essential if the focus is to be shifted to problems and away from countries, as such. It is one of the conditions which would allow a break to be made with the relationships which create feelings of dependence. There might be objections because suddenly some of the smallest countries are included in the large programs drawn up with the participation of their neighbors; but the creation of such ties is a goal in itself. Objections might also arise from the fact that the statutes of the World Bank would have to be changed because at present it can lend only with the guarantee of the governments concerned. However, it would all be well worthwhile if such changes meant a better focusing of external aid to particular regions and allowing it to transcend boundaries of countries too small to develop in isolation.

Methods of Distribution

It is, moreover, astonishing, even shocking and deplorable, that most of the responsibilities for the distribution of aid have not been entrusted to the developing countries themselves. When the United States launched the Marshall Plan, it took the decision—a highly statesmanlike one—to let Europe itself be responsible for distributing the funds among the different countries. The United States thus paved the way for the beginning of the European union; but what was more important at the time, it raised the aid receivers to a position of equality with the aid givers. And yet in our relations with the Third World, it is as if nothing had been learned from this lesson. One of the merits of the Punta del Este Charter which launched the Alliance for Progress was the institution of the committee of nine, which included only two North Americans, and which was to evaluate each country's programs and integrate them into an overall program. In effect, for the examination of each country's case, this committee divided itself into groups made up of three of its members and three outsiders. It had the wisdom in each case to apply for advice to at least one expert from outside the American continent—either from Europe or from some developing country—who could bring the benefits of original experience and sound objectivity to bear on the question. It remains to be seen to what extent the World Bank or even the various agencies of the United States have actually taken into account the propositions put forward by these groups, rather than relying on traditional criteria and choices. In fact, what has happened is that each Latin American country has remained in competition with the others and has done all it could to attract the benevolence of the American authorities and to obtain a more than proportional share of the financing.

One of the significant advantages of the special arrangement between the European Community and the African countries is that it brings the beneficiaries together for overall negotiations. For a long time things had been quite different. The aid of the European Development Fund was granted by the community and the only choice the African organization had was to accept. With the scarcity of some of the products supplied by certain African countries, the situation has begun to change. At any rate, for Latin America as much as for Africa one will have to get away from the old-style bilateral relationships—whether they be with the United States on the one hand or with the European Community, on the other.

It would not, of course, be realistic to imagine an organization taking over, for the whole of the Third World, the negotiation and the distribution of aid, as a European organization did for the Marshall Plan. To do so would be to combine too many different situations and would only accentuate a split between rich and poor countries. But there obviously is an important task here for regional groupings composed of neighboring countries at similar stages of development; providing that they are in a position to deal with aid givers of different origins. It would be most important to transfer to them some responsibility for the distribution among their members of aid and financial assistance from more diverse sources.

This would be one of the means of making sure that funds granted on the most favorable terms go to the least developed countries of all. For instance, the Andean group accords special facilities to Bolivia.

However, let there be no illusions on this score. Clearer principles and coordination between donors, and giving regional responsibilities to groups of beneficiary countries might go some way to helping the poorest countries or the poorest groups within a country; but in the end it is still the action of each developing country which will determine whether growth will happen, as it has in the past—through the maintenance or worsening of inequities— or through a real emphasis on reducing the greatest poverty. In the final analysis, it depends on what sort of markets are built up. If production is aimed at the privileged classes, it will perpetuate itself, its profits in turn maintaining the demand for its products. An entirely different pattern is not impossible. A circuit can be built up in which production is directed towards the nation's basic needs. It can be done through planning or through public enterprises, and through the appropriate manipulation of taxation. Eventually budgets, taxation, and the distribution of incomes should all contribute to reducing the inequalities. This is what is primarily at stake. For no country, the underdeveloped even less than the developed, can avoid making a choice, either explicitly in favor of a reduction of inequalities or, implicitly, to ignore them. The option is all the more acute today as a result of that other form of financial flows, private foreign investment, predominantly under the guise of multinational enterprises.

The subject of multinational enterprises (MNEs) cannot be approached dispassionately. The behavior of some of them—in Chile, Katanga, earlier in Central America, a scandal of corruption in the Italian oil industry, the creation of cartel agreements—have all led to a bad reputation for them. The developing countries congratulate themselves for having succeeded in getting the epithet "transnational" adopted in U.N. records. The more common adjective had the misfortune of being coined by the president of one of the largest firms in the world and seemed to imply that these enterprises not only operate in several countries, but are also independent of any national base.

May one think that a simple change of prefix is all that is needed in order to avoid giving the impression that these companies which straddle several countries escape a particular national point of view, to show on the contrary that they are still attached to one country while extending their activities far beyond its boundaries? What is really meant is "ultra-national"—but this term would be even more ambiguous. This debate on terminology clarifies at least one basic idea: it is better to refer to enterprises rather than to firms. The very diffusion of business activities beyond national frontiers does not necessarily imply a corporation with public shares; others expand abroad also, for instance, private businesses whose shares are not publicly held, state enterprises—and ultimately, cooperatives.

The verbal disorder does not end here. One of the chapters of the paper presented by the 77 developing countries at the conference on raw materials and development in April 1974 insisted on the urgent need to encourage and enlarge foreign investment, private as well as public. Another chapter deals with the controls and nationalization to which MNEs should be subject. As though private investment and MNEs were not practically one and the same thing, a number of emotional reactions of this sort have crept into the language of economics. The term "capital" arouses suspicions while "investment" is a term to be revered. As if capital were not simply the sum total of investment!

In fact the debate involving MNEs goes far beyond them. They are a means of attacking the whole idea of private enterprise, of private ownership of the means of production of which the MNEs represent extreme examples, the ultimate expression of the capitalist idea. The question is further confused by adding to it all the current worries about sustaining growth. Other arguments cite the MNEs in conjunction with the limitation of resources, the deterioration of the environment, and the dangers of pollution. The dangers of chemical or nuclear waste have very little to do with whether the producer's home base is national or multinational, whether a factory is public or private. Advertising which encourages wasteful consumption was not, after all, invented by the MNEs. The debate has by now been thoroughly confused; the MNE is blamed not only for what it does but also for a whole system for which it is the most glowing example.

What are the distinguishing characteristics of an MNE? To what extent can it be equated with direct private investment? Where is there a difference? What does an MNE have in common with any large-scale enterprise and what are its own special features?

DIRECT INVESTMENT

In the classical conception of things, little differentiation was made between international investment and capital transfers. Direct investment, for the most part, used to take the form of loans issued in the major financial centers. It was through these that the United States as well as Latin America were developed. One of our modern innovations is the distinction made between investment and capital movement. When firms install themselves in foreign countries, they draw some portion of their financial resources from the local market or from the banking system. At the time of the U.S. balance-of-payments deficits, American firms as of 1964 were openly encouraged to find funds overseas in order to avoid further increasing the deficit.

Direct investment is not itself a clearly defined idea. In the U.S. Department of Commerce statistics, this term is applied to the acquisition of more than 20 percent of shares in a business located outside the United States. This same criterion of 20 percent is used by the French government as the level at which foreign investment is brought under its control. The

United States tried to limit the amount of capital which flowed out of the country by imposing a tax (called an interest equalization tax) on foreign loans issued in the United States, as well as on the financing of American subsidiaries abroad. Firms were, however, allowed to avoid this tax if their share of a foreign firm's stock was greater than 10 percent.

One notion remains quite clear: direct investment is necessarily done by businesses. If an individual acquires a majority of shares in a company abroad, this remains simply portfolio investment. From there on it all depends on the degree of control that a firm has over another one in which it holds shares. Everything is clear-cut when the subsidiary is 100 percent owned. On the other hand, when participation is less than that, the local laws governing companies can have a decisive impact. The host country may require, for instance, that certain resolutions can only be carried by a qualified majority. Thus, even a majority would be insufficient, and a minority can be enough to block action. What is important to consider is how the rest of the capital is distributed. If it is spread widely, even a small holding can be enough to exercise control; if the remainder is closely grouped, on the other hand, even a majority can fail to give absolute control. Thus, before inferring a political significance from a foreign presence, one would have to examine, on a case-by-case basis, each subsidiary's capital structure in the widest sense of the word. This should then be analyzed in the light of prevailing commercial legislation, considering any other provisions which might work towards permitting a minority stockholder to exercise greater influence in the running of a foreign subsidiary. These include licensing and know-how agreements, management contracts, and understandings on when and how certain strategic decisions can be taken.

Even when all these nuances are taken into account, an MNE can still be synonymous with or distinct from direct investment; it usually depends on the definition which one chooses to adopt. In the case of a single investment, the distinction is clear. It is true that a sufficient number of isolated investments, by a sufficient number of firms, have their effect on capital movements, either in terms of inflows or, on the contrary, in terms of remittances abroad, of dividends, interest, and royalties. On the other hand, one can establish a kind of threshold as Ray Vernon has done. Here, the criterion is the existence of subsidiaries in at least six countries. This sort of definition has the advantage of reducing the sample, of creating a more homogeneous group, and making it possible to do useful analyses of structures and management methods. Thus, there is a tendency to seek a 100 percent takeover among those firms which manufacture the same products, automobiles, for example. Among firms with a variety of products, for example chemicals, there is a tendency to accept an association with local interests. It is clear that enterprises of this size and importance give rise to far more questions and even political tensions than does the average individual foreign investor. Many fears are expressed on all sides, by the MNEs' countries of origin as well as by the host countries, by the workers' representatives as well as by the MNEs themselves. These include anxieties about the disproportion between small and giant firms; about a supposed abundance of rapidly transferable capital; about the possibility of playing one union off against another and circumventing strikes in one country by increasing the deliveries from another. Other anxieties concern cultural change instigated as products copied from the most advanced technologies are implanted in less developed countries: distribution of markets, ways of manipulating the tax burden so firms will be taxed only in areas where taxation is lighter. Inversely, some of the fears concern the risks of arbitrary expropriation without adequate compensation. All this has led to a search for rules and procedures which would limit fears and negative effects. The fears indicate the need for a new framework to handle relations between governments and large corporations in such a way that all may cooperate in clearly defined ways. Thus, the economic contribution of the MNEs could be as great as possible, particularly in the developing countries.

Establishing businesses outside their countries of origin is not a new phenomenon by any means. What is relatively new is the increased rate and greater volume. In fact, there is an important distinction to be made here. Based in a developed but small country, an enterprise can only grow if it is multinational from the start. On the other hand, where the base is in a country which can itself offer a large market, notably the United States, the transition to multinational activity is usually a moving out from a well-established base.

PRUDENT EXTRAPOLATIONS

A certain amount of caution is required in the methods of calculating and making extrapolations about the part played by MNEs in the world's economy. One must avoid simply adding up total sales figures. Production is actually the sum of the "values added." Thus, one must deduct, from each organization's sales figures, internal transfers from one subsidiary to another. These should be counted only once—outside purchases should also be deducted. Furthermore, when a subsidiary is not 100 percent controlled, its part of the international overall production must be reduced in proportion to the investment which does not belong to the group concerned. Initial estimates of MNEs were based on a supposed relationship between the amount of capital involved and the amount of annual production. They applied this relationship to 100 percent control and reduced it by the appropriate coefficient, depending on the degrees of domestic participation. It would be better to use direct estimates which take into account, in addition to coefficients of participation, the value(s) added from each firm affiliated with the international group. The report of the Secretariat of the United Nations did not manage to do this. It was based on a supposed relationship between assets and value(s) added and it attributed to "international production," thus defined, a share of one-sixth of world industry.

In addition, it is generally thought that this international production grows twice as quickly as world production. This happens also to be the rate of development of international trade itself. Furthermore this lumps together enterprises that were multinational from the beginning and firms which entered this field after they had been purely national, even though exporters. Above all, it is important to beware of extrapolations which tend to conclude that all production will someday be accounted for by the MNEs or rather by a handful of them.

Thanks to general economic growth trends, as well as to a lessening of tariff barriers, world trade has expanded in an unprecedented way. Lower tariff barriers provide a twofold impetus for installing bridgeheads in prosperous markets and for surmounting remaining barriers to trade by production under their protection. The period during which the dollar was overvalued constituted a stimulant for American enterprises to produce abroad. The protests of U.S. unions against the export of jobs which this implied were but one more expression of the imbalance of exchange rates. Production costs were lower abroad even when differences of productivity and economies of scale were taken into account along with labor costs. It was further to be expected that the yield of investments would ultimately be collected in currencies, some of which were bound to rise in relation to the American. One cannot extrapolate over a long period the relationships of costs and expectations. These were largely adjusted by modifications in exchange rates; although the spectacular recovery of the dollar after a sudden fall might once again go beyond the long-term balance of costs. Everything in this area depends on government reaction, which is always hard to predict. There are those who will be more concerned than in the past, with limiting concentrations considered too excessive or dangerous for competition. On the other hand, there are governments which will continue to worry about excessive dependence upon foreign enterprises and about the large drains on their balance of payments if these firms repatriated their profits. Even at the level of some of the largest firms, company directors are considering changes of strategy. In their competition with each other, they had sought growth for the sake of growth, to the point where they were increasing their indebtedness. Now they are considering a more selective approach whereby a larger return on their resources would be drawn from a less extended field.

Large corporations and multinational enterprises (these terms are not necessarily synonymous) and the consequences of their activities might be quite distinct. When a firm finds itself all alone in a narrow national market, the tendency for it to become monopolistic is all the greater. In this case, the arrival of foreign firms is usually considered a threat, not for the monopolies they entail, but for the competition they will introduce in a stable situation. They may be more dynamic, more willing to pay higher wages; their higher profits will permit them to increase their share of the market. Such are the fears that have revived protectionist tendencies in a number of European countries which, having let up little by little on their protection against the entry of foreign products, now feel a need to protect themselves against the entry of foreign firms. A takeover of an entire sector by a foreign firm, that is, a monopoly by a foreign power, would be an extreme case and could only happen within one of the advanced technologies. As for the question whether big foreign firms are more inclined to create a demand for certain products, rather then creating products to supply demand, this is not an activity peculiar to MNEs; it is part of the basic criticisms leveled at the way the market functions in modern economies. Nevertheless, it is true to say that advertising and brand names do produce increasing returns; their use is all the more effective, therefore, when it covers a larger number of markets.

Once one gets to the heart of the matter, one sees that the growth of MNEs shows up three distinct sorts of contradictions. First, there is a contradiction between the internationalization of business and partitioning sustained by national governments. Second, there is also a contradiction between the needs of different countries for this type of investment and their capacity to remain masters of it. Finally, there is a contradiction between two sorts of correlation: that of the rate of growth associated with the presence of MNEs but also that of the spreading of inequalities associated with it. Each of these contradictions requires a separate analysis.

INTERNATIONAL BUSINESS
AND GOVERNMENT PARTITIONING

As regards the first conflict, the developed countries and the developing countries are in the same boat. We have only to consider the three areas in which national sovereignty particularly seeks to assert itself. The first is the field of taxation to which we will return later at greater length. For now, it is enough to point out that the disparity of rates and rules of assessment for companies sometimes puts the MNEs in the position where they have to risk double taxation, or on the contrary, at other times, allows them to declare their profits in tax havens or other places where they will be less heavily taxed. There is no general rule, no practical coordination to prevent such distortions. Furthermore, if a country tries to regulate credit as part of its fight against inflation or of its effort to develop investments selectively, its attempts run the risk of being circumvented by recourse to the international finance market. A country might well encourage its own firms, to the degree that they are national, to resort to external credits or, on the contrary, it might forbid them to do so. MNEs can do without encouragements and can twist most prohibitions. Within their common financial base, they can always release funds there where they must not appear to have been borrowed, even if that means borrowing them in a place where the same restrictions do not apply. This all goes to show that an essential instrument of monetary policy has lost its effectiveness. Furthermore, one must not forget that MNEs have considerable funds at their disposal. They are suspected of transferring funds from one currency to another following interest rates, or even better, can anticipate ups and downs in particular exchange rates. To lay all this at the doorstep of the MNEs is, of course, almost tantamount to accusing them of being responsible for international speculation. But it is too easy to confuse short-term assets with liquidities; a large part of the working balance of a firm is made up of commercial bills—either payable or receivable—while another part must be available at all times for urgent expenditures. The margin is smaller than one might imagine, and it would not do to confuse cause and effect. The convertibility of currencies was established without sufficient thought being given to even the slightest coordination in the policies of the central banks. Interest rates are manipulated, more to fill the gaps in public finance policies than to take account of balance-of-payments situations. This is the case despite the fact that interest rates should be raised to attract capital in times of deficit and lowered in times of surplus. As long as states will not stabilize their currencies, it is only natural that the financial managers of companies will take steps to avoid losses. One of the great monetary experts, Edward Bernstein, has analyzed American data and discovered that at the time when the mark, the yen, and the dollar were going through great crises, transfers of funds by companies were in fact much smaller than might have been imagined. His ironical conclusion was that the treasurers weren't yet used to the game and that they would undoubtedly do better next time.

Hence, instead of the MNEs being choice instruments for the rational worldwide distribution of resources, it is the lack of coordination between governments which leads to the worst distortions. This is all the more so as each government prides itself on having an industrial policy, which is really nothing more than a glorified title for disparate measures which in most cases do not fit into any kind of coherent logic. Taken in its most constructive sense, an industrial policy must satisfy a basic requirement: the preparation and implementation of investment decisions extend over a long period and should not be based on the factors of competition, price and profit prevailing at one point in time. In other words, beyond immediate comparative advantages, investors should be concerned with potential advantages. There is a big difference between an industry just starting out in a place without infrastructure, without either suppliers or customers at hand, and the industry which it will become once it has benefited from both economies of scale and external economies. It is one thing to offer initial protection which will disappear over time, and quite another to institutionalize such protective measures and subsidies. A proper industrial policy would define its criteria for relations between large and small enterprises, between the private and public sectors. In fact this day is far off; pressures and chance count far more than the finest calculations. The disorder that exists at present only serves to encourage MNEs to lead states into competition between themselves, to play on promised advantages, and to get around obstacles that some states have set up.

BARGAINING POWER

The second consideration in the growth of MNEs is the need for foreign investment. Even the most developed countries benefit from the technology and competition created by those firms whose management is the most rational or the most advanced. In this sense, the more under-developed a country is, the more it gains from investment. However, to the extent that a country is small, its government weak, its administration lacking in cohesion, the less it is capable of dealing with large foreign enterprises on an equal footing. There is no lack of examples of enterprises being attracted by special conditions destined to overcome initial risks and narrow market outlets. It is precisely this kind of situation which has most often led to later difficulties; for no sooner is the deal concluded, than the government begins to regret the concessions it has made. Industries would do well to ask for nothing beyond a strict application of the law. The clearer the development plans of the host country, the better, of course, a foreign company will be able to size up the environment in which it is to establish itself. This is no easy task for less developed countries

(LDCs), for even the most advanced countries are barely able to make plans and often find it much easier to abandon them, than to execute them or adapt them to circumstances.

States often have the mistaken idea that it is the very foreignness of an enterprise which allows it to escape from their authority. In fact, governmental power is enough to impose national goals upon firms anywhere; in this sense control is different from ownership. The American government does not have any less authority over public services carried out by private companies than it would have if they were nationalized; the same is true for suppliers of government orders. If a country wants to hold stock in a firm, this should be less of an attempt to control it but primarily because it wants to share in the profits. Rules governing foreign companies must be clearly fixed from the beginning; for example a firm should know whether and for how long certain protection may be accorded or certain restrictions accepted on its exports. Alternatively, there could be explicit clauses allowing for revision of contracts, either at regular intervals or when circumstances have clearly changed. The creation of regional markets is a case in point. Major obstacles to regional integration can arise from clauses in existing contracts between MNEs and member countries or where MNEs have signed licensing agreements limiting exports so that they would not compete with other subsidiaries or license beneficiaries. The rule implicit in every contract, which in legal language is called *rebus sic stantibus,* must allow for the removal of such restrictions which work against the integration without at the same time giving rise to accusations of retroactive legislation.

The European experience shows to what degree it is necessary for a regional union to elaborate a common policy with regard to foreign investment. Even after 15 years as a union some Commom Market countries were still following restrictive policies, while others were outbidding each other on concessions and lures designed to attract foreign firms. In fact this produces the strangest distortions: a member applying restrictions finds them circumvented by its partner's policies; unwanted goods find their way to its territory without allowing it to benefit from either the production or the employment. On the other hand, there has been a real escalation in concessions; to the point where certain countries use foreign firms as a privileged instrument for competition with their own partners.

In a more general sense, Third World countries entertain very divergent attitudes about MNEs. Some countries attract them while others remain suspicious. The result is much unevenness in the distribution of MNE activities. From a global point of view policies likely to succeed should avoid excessive restrictions which others refuse, and similarly avoid total laissez-faire to which others do not adhere. A second component of such policies would be the opening of a common path whereby MNEs can make their greatest contribution to development wherever they install themselves.

GROWTH AND INEQUALITIES

However, one must now face a third consideration: it would be well to know just what can be expected of these MNEs and what remains beyond their capacity. A chapter written by the OECD Secretariat, for a study edited by Reuben on private international investment, seems to confirm the correlation between the presence of an MNE and general rates of growth. The correlation seemed more marked than in the case of overall financial flows, to the extent that only in a small number of countries (themselves quite small) had such flows reached a scale where they played a determining role in growth. The diagram above (See Figure 3) confirms this analysis. But so general a relationship does not show anything about the distribution of investment, nor about its internal effects. On the whole, four-fifths of all MNE investments take place in the most industrialized countries. Those which go to developing countries for the most part go where per capita income is relatively high, or where the population is sufficiently large, or where there are exploitable natural resources. This correlation of the investment flows with the level of per capita income comes out quite clearly in the diagram (See Figure 4). In other words, it is unavoidable that private investment widens the gulf between developed and developing countries, as well as between developing countries themselves. The smallest and poorest have no facilities for receiving MNEs. To think that as public aid diminishes, private investment can take over, is thus a great mistake. It is tantamount to supposing that within a given country, even a developed one, investments will of their own accord fill the gaps in backward or declining areas. It is only through transfers of revenue controlled by government, through the establishment of basic facilities upon which profitable investments can build, that a certain equalization can come about. The same is true on a worldwide scale: for the poorest countries private investment and the MNEs themselves can do little.

Even for the less poor countries, other means are needed to insure the development of basic infrastructures. This means that the more private investment there is in the world, the more necessary increased aid becomes, otherwise development will be all the more uneven and warped.

The effect of inequality is not only to be found between countries, but is inevitable even within developing countries themselves. For when a highly productive firm arrives on the scene, it does not immediately spread its effects evenly over the whole of the economy. In some cases such a firm will pay higher wages than those currently being paid, and thus at the outset, at least, create a privileged group. In industrialized countries, unions often forget that the relation between industrial wages and other incomes is reversed in the developing world. Wage earners in industrialized countries generally have an income inferior to those of other categories; whereas in underdeveloped countries their revenue may be a multiple of that of small farmers. Moreover, the products introduced by a new firm are more likely to be consumed by the better-off part of the society. The insistence of many states on joint ventures rather than on pure subsidiaries may also contribute to an unevenness of incomes. The development of local financial markets is not within reach of all developing countries, and in any case it would be accessible only to a small part of the population. This basic situation justifies all the more the setting up of joint ventures with the developing country's government participation, rather than with that of vintage capitalists. The constant preoccupation, both of the MNE's country of origin and the host country, should be to provide financial means for making up for the inequalities caused by the introduction of a foreign firm in an underdeveloped economy.

Conflicting Views

Thus any analysis of the advantages brought to an underdeveloped country by the establishment of an MNE is fraught with serious problems of appreciation. The simplest way of looking at it is merely to note the inflow of capital and technology, and the tax receipts from these new taxpayers. The obvious retort is equally simplistic: that is, any foreign investment has two phases, the inflow of capital and the repatriation of profits. It goes without saying that in any situation of profitable investment there are more exits than entries, which results in a drain on the balance of payments. As for taxes, one must first examine whatever special concessions may have been granted or whether the companies in question are not bypassing local taxation through transfers of profits to tax havens. On the balance-of-payments questions the eulogists would reply that one must look beyond the mere entry and exit of funds. The extreme form of the argument was presented by Herbert May in a document drawn up for the Council of the Americas. Not only did he ascribe to foreign enterprises the exports for which they are responsible—which at first glance is quite legitimate—but he went so far as to consider all their additional production as equivalent to a saving on imports. Here the argument becomes quite contradictory, for a country can obviously only import if it produces, that is to say if it creates revenues which in their turn create demand. Even where production is a substitute for imports, it is not necessarily a saving on imports; one must first take a closer look at the extra imports which were necessary for the added production. Quite clearly the effects of foreign investments on economic growth, balance of payments, and public finance, include pluses and minuses which must be added up by comparing them with the possible effects of purely domestic investment insofar as such an option exists.

If, as often happens, the foreign enterprise borrows a part of its funds locally, the pressure on the balance of payments is likely to be all the greater. In fact the very profits which will be repatriated do not necessarily have any connection with the capital brought in from outside. It is for this reason that Argentina has decided that foreign companies wishing to invest there will be obliged to import all their funds; they will be able to export them only insofar as they come from outside. Paul Rostenstein Rodan has argued that the rate of return on investment is usually higher than the rate of interest on loans. In the nineteenth century Latin America thus obtained a large proportion of necessary capital in the form of government loans or by bonds issued on the large money markets. Nowadays, direct investments there must pay off—the cost is higher than that of loans. Rodan thus considers that direct investment or equity financing should in some cases be accompanied by loans from the MNE's country of origin and in a proportion to be defined. Such a solution could lighten the burden for the developing countries. It would in effect reproduce the leverage that normally obtains when a firm finances part of its investments through loans. In fact it is not always possible to link together investments to such a fixed-interest base of capital. It is only one formula among others to prevent the servicing of capital from becoming too great a strain on the balance of payments. What can be most inconvenient is that the burden of debt remains unchanged during the periods when the value of exports diminishes, especially after a lessening in demand affects both quantities and prices. Profit transfers, on the other hand, are much more flexible, and naturally decline with a lessening of activity brought about by a lowering of exports.

Albert Hirschman, in a pamphlet on the need for the United States to give up investment in Latin America, goes straight to the heart of the matter. He raises doubts even about the internal effect of foreign enterprises. He considers that they constitute an easy way out for Latin American countries, but that at the same time they create obstacles to the development of local savings and entrepreneurship. He notes that during those periods—notably during the great wars—when certain countries were obliged to cut down on their financial assets abroad, the Latin Americans had no trouble at all in mustering the necessary funds to buy them back. True enough, foreign firms do hire most of their personnel in the host country even to fill the responsible positions. The fact remains that a subsidiary does not pose the same problems, where final decisions are concerned, as an independent firm. In other words, foreign enterprises are likely to compete with the development of local ones without giving Latin Americans the kind of training which is the essence of management—the strategy of decision making. Hirschman has made a number of proposals to help avoid frictions produced by the presence of foreign enterprises or brutal reactions which could lead to open conflict. One of his suggestions is that there be an international organization, regularly supplied with funds from the developed countries, which would take charge temporarily of the capital which developing states are not able immediately to reimburse.

There is nothing outrageous in the idea that foreign ownership should be gradually reduced in an economy. The United States is a case in point: it has been estimated that at the end of the nineteenth century foreign capital represented 15 percent of total capital assets; today this has been reduced to 1 percent at the most, either through buying back or through wartime confiscations of enemy property. The reduction of the relative portion does not necessarily mean disinvestment, expropriation, or repayment—it is enough if, insofar as an enterprise's capital grows, the foreign share should grow little or not at all. American telephone companies, for instance, once owned 100 percent of a subsidiary in Canada, but because they did not follow capital increases, their participation today is reduced to 3 percent. Nevertheless Hirschman's plan is based on assumptions which are not explicit. The first is that the necessary domestic savings always exist to take the place of foreign capital. The second is that local entrepreneurs will arise and will be ready to take risks. While this may be so in some Latin American countries, it is obviously true to a lesser extent in other countries, on other continents. A warning sounded by Ray Vernon* should be borne in mind: the substitution of local enterprises for foreign ones is not only likely to cut off certain inflows of capital, but also to undo precious links which can provide a constant supply of technological progress, management ability, and marketing techniques.

An Objective Analysis

The problem is that such opposing points of view do not provide a clear picture of what the benefits and costs of foreign ownership really are;

---

*Sovereignty at Bay: The Multinational Spread of U.S. Enterprises (New York: Basic Books, 1971).

to attempt a more careful analysis, however, would probably be to run into serious insufficiencies of data. In a report to the OECD Development Center, Bos has tried to show all the factors which must be taken into consideration if one is to avoid oversimplification and errors of judgement. Entries and exits of capital must be taken into account, of course, but so must local reinvestment insofar as it constitutes added capital and helps prevent borrowing from abroad. However, even this type of outside saving cannot be counted in its entirety without first examining whether in its absence it might not have been replaced by domestic savings. In the same way exports attributable to MNEs should only be counted to the extent to which they exceed what a purely local company might have exported; after all, if the import content of such exports were measured, the balance might well turn out to be negative, particularly if comparisons are made with alternative domestic solutions. Similarly, the impact on public finance must be measured in terms of taxes paid as well as subsidies received by a local firm. Nor do the calculations end there. One must try to get as complete a picture as possible of the overall economic stimulation provided by the establishment of a firm, the various activities it gives rise to by, for example, giving work to local suppliers, or by introducing goods and services destined to be consumed by those it employs. For, quite to the contrary, an enterprise can remain almost entirely apart from the rest of a society; indeed its very modernity can be a hindrance to the development of the rest of the economy.

This enclave situation has long been a characteristic of the oil companies. In Venezuela, for example, one might well ask whether the salaries the oil industry could pay, the external receipts it brought in, did not lead to a rate of exchange and a level of return on capital which made more difficult the creation of other industries capable of competing with the outside. Indeed, Venezuela took a very long time in accepting free trade agreements which are beginning to take root in Latin America. Yet it is only fair to say that this same contradiction may apply just as well to purely national investment. The Algerian experience will be interesting in this regard. Will the energetic efforts being made to create petrochemical and iron smelting industries have "spin-off" effects on other activities? Is it not possible that such as advanced sector will be unable to create enough jobs, will not find enough outlets for its production, will absorb resources which should have been used for the development of more modest economic activities? This kind of dichotomy is often a serious obstacle to development. Maybe one of the keys to the Japanese economic success is in the original nature of its employment system which avoided the effects of such a dichotomy. Lifetime employment in large firms, although it attracts labor from traditional sectors and enterprises, also acts as a barrier to too heavy a drain from these sectors. In this way it

avoids pulling salaries upwards in sectors where productivity is not
sufficient to cover them. In situations where no such barriers exist
traditional sectors and the jobs they provide may wither away. The risk of
this kind of situation is no less great in new industries geared for
exporting than it is for those engaged in import substitution sheltered by
protection.

These analyses and examples should serve to clear the air of excessive
simplifications and the impassioned attitudes they give rise to. But quite
obviously not every appraisal can be based on figures, especially since an
understanding of internal alternative solutions and their possible spin-off
or braking effects involve such a large amount of guesswork. In practice the
calculations based on cost-benefit formulas, both real and hypothetical, are
never strictly accurate. But by taking all factors into account, one can
arrive at a kind of policy of probabilities, that is, to develop formulas for
increasing the advantages and diminishing the costs of MNEs.

A PROBABILIST POLICY

Let us review the conditions which should be met in developing a
probabilist policy: a positive contribution to the balance of payments,
better than one that could be obtained through a purely internal solution;
more rapid, more stable, and above all better distributed growth; finally,
what is to be avoided is the stifling effect that the presence of foreign
enterprises may have on local savings, entrepreneurship, and management
capacity.

In Latin America there has been an initiative, taken jointly by large
firms which tried to respond to both the above realities and the requirements; it was followed by similar efforts in Asia and later in Africa.

The first principle in these efforts is to create a company which is
actually multinational, to replace direct investment by separate enterprises. The capital is subscribed by large companies from the United
States, from several countries in Europe, and also from Japan. In order to
create real interest, no share may be less than $100,000; nor more than
$500,000, to avoid the development of dominant influences. The second
principle is to accept only minority shareholding, to agree on a Latin
American majority, which is to be responsible, as much as possible, for the
management. The third principle is to make use of the financial standing
of these large firms to ease complementary financing through loans or
credit. The fourth principle is to diminish progressively the shares taken in
such enterprises in order to release funds which may be invested in new
ventures. The fifth, and perhaps most important, is to be oriented towards

sectors in which this type of cooperation can be most fruitful for the countries concerned, and to conciliate in this way the profitability of investment with the contribution to development.

Thus the effects of any domination by a foreign enterprise can be nipped in the bud. Far from placing any obstacles in the way of the formation of domestic capital or to the development of management capability, these mechanisms would encourage and facilitate them. Especially since the advice and experience of the largest firms in the world would be available. In the end there would be no great burden on the balance of payments for in proportion as the capital is returned to the local interests, it would become available for new ventures.

However successful the experiment, known as the ADELA (Allocation for the Development of Latin America), has been, it is self-evident that this model cannot be applied generally. It cannot be stretched to the point where it would become a substitute for other forms of foreign investment, nor for the creation of MNE subsidiaries. Nevertheless it should be possible to preserve elsewhere several features of this initiative.

A great part of the political difficulties associated with international investment stems from the identification of a subsidiary with a foreign company and thus with the country to which it belongs. The dominance of American firms in Latin America may well be followed by a similar European dominance in Africa and, willy-nilly, Japan's assuming the same position in Asia. However, legislation in some developing countries is showing the way. Mexico, for example, insists upon a national majority share in firms; in fact, it has raised the minimum from 51 percent to 60 percent. A minority share will nonetheless be tolerated where the rest of the capital belongs to firms from several different countries. This policy is in effect a good bet, because there is no reason to suppose that the foreign investors would form a bloc, and, after all, alliances can be formed as easily between national and foreign participants. A definite effort should be made to insure that foreign investment in general be undertaken jointly by the firms of several nationalities and, where possible, from different continents.

It would be preferable that for their part, the host countries defined well in advance at what moment they meant to take a share—either governmental or by local capitalists—if the firms which come from abroad indicate at what point they would insist on participation by their nationals in the personnel and management of these firms. It would be natural too, that the host countries outlined the sectors to which they would prefer to see foreign capital directed subsequently, as the initial investments are gradually replaced by local capital. Such schemes could prevent misunderstandings and tensions, and could make of foreign enterprises a real impetus for a balanced, and less dependent, national development.

6

MNEs could serve as bridgeheads for a better division of labor, more egalitarian development, and even for a democratic organization of labor. Sweden has set a useful example with a system of insurance against the risks of investment abroad, by making the granting of guarantees subject to certain rules which the firms have to follow. In reality this system is very complex and, as none of the Swedish firms has ever come up against any great difficulties, the guarantees have never actually been put into practice. The United States has set up an Overseas Private Investment Corporation which offers American investors abroad, in return for a small commission, guarantees against the risk of inadequate compensation in case of expropriation. The corporation set an example when it refused the benefits of this insurance to ITT after it was revealed that the latter had attempted to intervene against a democratically elected government in Chile. The Commission of the European Community, in its turn, is considering the rules it would like to impose on the MNEs which come under its jurisdiction

Almost all the MNEs have originated in the United States, in the European Community, or, to a lesser degree, in Japan. Coordinated action on the part of all three of these, or even on the part of one alone, say the European Community, could considerably improve the role of MNEs and their relations with their host countries. However, if such initiatives, well intentioned as they may be, are not to appear to other states as outside interventions in their affairs, they must be made clear to, and concerted with the developing countries. The group formed by the United Nations to study the impact of MNEs on development and on international relations has proposed that the Economic and Social Council (ECOSOC) regularly examine these problems, and be assisted in this task by an independent commission together with a center for research and information. Such an arrangement might well provide the necessary forum for this type of consultation.

All things considered, the areas that count most are taxation, market conditions, and labor relations.

THE TAX JUNGLE

Taxation has always seemed to be an especially dry subject; the general public never gives it the attention it deserves. As a result, certain interests often manage to gain ground and reap advantages, which are paid for by the unwitting masses.

One example will help to reveal the significance of some tax arrangements. For a long time now, American oil companies have been allowed by the U.S. government to consider the royalties they pay to the oil producing states as taxes on their profits and thus to deduct them from taxes owed to the American treasury. Consequently, the American administration has scarcely ever received anything from these companies, which were induced all along to develop their pursuits abroad. Today the whole world is paying the price of this policy. It is true, on the other hand, that American tax laws include a clause unknown anywhere else: all countries allow for depreciation on equipment, but the American tax authorities also make provision for the depletion of natural resources. Add to this the fact that private investment in petroleum research benefits from the kind of tax exemptions which are generally used to limit progressive taxation on the highest incomes, and one has a situation where firms receive encouragement to invest both abroad and at home; it is up to them to even things out, and up to all the other taxpayers to bear the burden of all those taxes the firms are exempted from in one way or another.

Quite obviously, for the MNEs the disparity of different countries' tax laws is a source of complication and confusion. There are clauses favoring investment abroad over local investment; conversely there are clauses more favorable to internal investment. Furthermore, the relationship between taxes paid in the country of origin and in the host country usually allows for two types of situation: double taxation, unfavorable to investment abroad, on the one hand, or savings on overall taxation, (especially through tax haven channels), on the other. The economic decisions of the MNEs are generally distorted by the constant search for the lowest tax burden; this is, moreover, one of the factors which underlies price manipulation on transfers of goods or services between affiliates of the same network. A disorderly competition thus develops between the stronger and weaker countries to attract investment through concessions, the main cost of which is in effect borne by the wage earners in the developed countries or the poorest peasants in the LDCs. Such goings-on merit that public attention overcome its repugnance for these, seemingly, too technical problems.

The different taxation systems involved and how they affect various activities, as well as contributions to development, are all questions which can be set out in relatively simple terms. The truth of the matter is that there are not even generally accepted rules by which the nationality of a firm can be determined, in other words, its country of origin—is it where its head office is registered or is it where its effective headquarters are located? Of course the rate at which companies are taxed varies widely, especially among developing countries—some have the highest rates of taxation in the world, some the lowest—whereas among developed countries tax rates tend to converge in the neighborhood of 50 percent. One must, of course, look more closely at tax bases of assessment, allowable deductions, and the method by which they are calculated.

The greatest complications arise from the two levels at which corporate income can be treated: at the level of the company and that of the individual shareholder. The classic system, which obtains in the United States and Japan, allows for a double taxation; in other words, the companies are taxed on their profits, and the shareholder according to his share of the revenue, that is, on the dividends he receives. Other countries, like Germany, apply two rates at the company level: the distribution of profits is encouraged by a lower rate of taxation on the part of company revenue which is issued in dividends. France has chosen a more complex technique: the shareholder benefits from a tax credit, which is considered to represent a part of the taxes paid by the company itself, and which is supposed to act as a kind of advance deduction; this advantage is, however, reserved for residents of France or those of certain countries with which it has bilateral agreements. Foreign firms which receive dividends are thus unlikely to benefit from this deduction. On the other hand, internally, the French state in some cases may find itself paying a negative tax to shareholders; if their dividends, for instance, are taxed at a lower rate than the equivalent of the tax credit. In practice, the state in fact pays out when a shareholder's tax does not exceed one-third of his revenue. Generally speaking in developing countries and in some developed countries too, remittances abroad are usually subjected to a withholding tax, the justification for this being that internal beneficiaries pay personal taxes on their incomes. It is clear, however, that such a system is more likely to encourage investment through loans rather than through capital contributions, because the withholding tax on interests is applied only at the moment when they are transferred abroad, whereas direct capital also pays local taxes on the profits.

From this preliminary information one already gets a fair idea of the great diversity of the constraints as well as the loopholes within which MNEs work. To these one must add the many different ways in which the countries of origin treat revenues earned abroad and revenues earned at home.

An extreme practice is one which takes only those profits realized on the territory of the country of origin and completely omits those earned elsewhere. France is one of the countries which applies this principle: indeed France has gone even further in that it does not oblige its firms to consolidate its external and domestic profits; on the other hand it allows deductions for certain early losses in foreign investment. In other words foreign profits are not added to those made in France, but foreign losses are deducted. Nonetheless, tax payments based on overall profits are always another option: certain firms adopt this solution when they find it to their advantage because of extra deductions. The other extreme would be taxation by a country of origin on a worldwide scale, but this absolute form of system is not enforced anywhere yet. Its application is envisaged in Canada, ruling out the deduction of taxes paid elsewhere unless it is provided by bilateral agreements on the avoidance of double taxation. Canadian firms, of course, protested against this system which would only be applied to them, and which would make double taxation the rule and tax deductions the exception. The most common practice is to tax all profits on a worldwide scale, at least in theory, but in practice to tax external gains only if and when they are repatriated. This acts as an incentive to reinvest locally in countries where taxation rates are lower; double taxation occurs only rarely; in most cases it is avoided by bilateral treaties or by unilateral action on the part of the MNE's country of origin. This is the usual procedure followed by the United States.

Extraordinary though this jungle may seem, it nevertheless reveals certain effects. There is a proliferation of tax havens, places where taxation is nil or purely nominal. Inversely, double taxation is not altogether eliminated; the conventions that exist are mainly between developed countries where capital moves in both directions and each country is prompted to take into account the taxes paid elsewhere by its residents, in exchange for advantages given to residents of the other country so that they will not be discouraged from investing in the first. However, in underdeveloped countries capital movements are in one direction only. When developing countries play off one against the other, accord special tax concessions to foreign firms, or simply allow them to benefit from normal local preferential investment facilities, they often discover that they draw little if any benefit from it, for the receipts which they deliberately forego are usually taken over, either immediately or in time, by the MNE's country of origin. Moreover, the means at the disposal of the developing countries to attract investment can rarely compete with the concessions which the rich countries can offer.

THREE OBJECTIVES

There are three goals to be aimed for in the search for coordination of tax laws. The elimination of tax evasion, especially through tax havens; the suppression of double taxation; and the avoidance of differences in rates depending on the form the capital movement takes—these three combined could contribute to development, not only in terms of growth but also in terms of a reduction of inequalities.

In the light of these objectives one must examine various proposals for reform as well as the main practices of the home countries of foreign investors as regards the investments of their firms abroad.

Vernon's reaction to the size and proportion of modern MNE activities is to suggest that all countries in which each MNE operates should have a share in that MNE's overall profits. In other words, overall profits should be distributed generally among the countries concerned rather than by virtue of where different accounting practices have allowed certain profits to show up. In this way the urge to move profits, to manipulate prices, would be eliminated; investments would be motivated by cost and profitability without being warped by tax considerations. However, this proposal, generous as it may be, comes up against a disheartening experience. In the United States a number of states levy a tax on companies, over and above the federal tax. These states thus claim a part of a firm's consolidated profits and define their share by the firm's combined turnover, employment, and assets situated in the state compared with the whole of the country. No agreement has ever been reached, however, by the different states to use the same formula so that the distribution would be equitable. It is not hard to see the infinitely greater difficulty in applying such a system on an international scale, all the more so since the sums involved are so much greater than the mere taxes imposed on firms by local communities. There is, furthermore, an ambiguity: if it is the overall profits of a firm that are to be divided by agreement, each state that benefits from this sharing remains free to impose its own rates in its own way; there would be no end to the disorganized competition that would ensue. How can an overall tax levy be divided when taxation rates and tax bases are not the same everywhere? This ambitious plan is not, therefore, likely to achieve its purposes, nor their practical requirements.

Another scheme which has the support of a large number of economists is envisaged by the Commission of the European Community;

it has even been submitted as a legislative bill in the United States. The principle would be that each country of origin taxes its MNEs on their overall profits, as if these had been earned within the country, but deducts such taxes as the MNEs have to pay in other countries. This differs in two ways from current practices: taxation takes place as soon as the profits are earned, without waiting for them to be repatriated; the elimination of double taxation becomes a matter of course without any need for special arrangements or bilateral agreements. The theory behind such a system is that it would make investment decisions as independent as possible from the various taxation laws. Tax havens would naturally lose their attraction. The less a firm is taxed abroad, the more it would have to pay at home! As for the developing countries, their negotiating powers would be strengthened; for firms would gain nothing through special concessions which would be cancelled out by the higher taxes they would be obliged to pay in their countries of origin. By the same token developing countries would be encouraged to raise their taxation rates to resemble those which generally prevail in developed countries; and in this way would obtain the financial means to cover the costs of establishing infrastructures and making up for inequalities.

Obviously such a system demands the broadest possible information on the activities of any multinational group. But it would enhance the interest governments have in obtaining and releasing such information; information which is, after all, essential to the levying of taxes, as well as to enabling host countries to judge the advantages and costs of competing offers and projects, and finally, so that all those affected by a firm's activities—shareholders, employees, suppliers, and customers—may understand its management practices and fight against any discrimination. Needless to say, a consolidation of profits is particularly difficult in periods of monetary instability and abrupt variations in exchange rates; it remains, nonetheless, indispensable to any efficient management.

Two objections in passing: one was brought up by the American administration in the Trade Reform Bill of 1975 with which it armed itself for the multilateral trade negotiations. It was noted that the end result would be that companies of different origins, operating in the same country, would be taxed at different rates, depending on the taxation laws in effect in their respective countries of origin. Nevertheless, the system itself would create a tendency to uniformity which, if it were generally applied, would rule out this difficulty. On the other hand, what should be given careful attention are not the particular encouragements given to foreign firms, but those generally offered to foreign or local firms alike to favor investment: whether it is with a view to stabilizing the economy, accelerating growth, making up for initial disadvantages, or assuring a better regional balance. Unless complementary arrangements were made, the scheme under consideration would end up reserving for local firms the benefits of these general arrangements, to the exclusion of foreign firms which could, on the contrary, benefit from such advantages in their home countries. The imbalance between underdeveloped and developed countries would then only be aggravated.

Thus the difficulties speak for themselves. Provided, however, appropriate corrections are built in, a system of overall taxation at the time when the revenue is earned and with deductions made for taxes paid elsewhere, seems to be the best. It will take time, of course, before it is applied by all the major investing countries. In the meantime a U.N. committee of tax experts has begun work on the question. They have tried to set up a model agreement on the avoidance of double taxation, to establish in this way a point of reference for developing countries to invoke in their negotiations with the developed countries. One may fear that the repaired number of such bilateral accords will prove to be discouraging and that, however uniform the main aspects, significant differences will subsist about the rates of withholding tax which countries of origin would accept as deductions. Thus the distortions would not be completely eliminated. The U.N. group has expressed the hope that such efforts would be speeded up and that whatever arrangements are decided upon, they would be uniform enough to amount to an international agreement on taxation.

PRACTICAL STEPS

What is most urgent is to determine what special measures should be devised to complement any system that is eventually set up to attain the aforementioned threefold objective of reducing tax evasion, suppressing distortions, and bringing a greater contribution to development.

Tax havens, where many MNEs establish holdings which govern their foreign activities, are one of the most dubious facilities within a competitive system. Until now, governments have in many cases been in favor of their own enterprises availing themselves of these, under the pretext that their firms would otherwise be disadvantaged in comparison with other firms. In this way, various countries all encourage each other to take the easy way out. This unfortunate tendency must be reversed! The advantages MNEs derive from their very size, their organization, their information network, and their marketing techniques, are more than enough; there is no need for them to benefit from abnormal facilities as well. In fact the MNEs would gain by having such suspicions dissolved. It goes without saying that as long as tax havens exist, each firm will feel

---

compelled to benefit from them; if it didn't its stockholders would want to know why their firm doesn't resort to the methods of its competitors to increase their profits. The elimination of such possibilities, by all countries of origin acting in concert, would thus have a salutary effect upon a situation which is quite contrary to ideas of fair play and, in the last analysis, to the disadvantage of the MNEs' image.

For the elimination of tax havens, a system of direct taxation on a worldwide scale would be the most effective. The less any firm paid to Liechtenstein or the Bahamas, the more it would owe to Washington or London. When outside profits are taxed only at the time of repatriation, it is, of course, of considerable advantage to keep them for as long as possible in one of these fiscal gardens of Eden. The Trade Reform Act provides for a complicated procedure whereby taxes would be slapped on immediately where it can be proved that funds are not being repatriated in order to reduce the tax burden. A more effective formula would be to tax profits immediately as they leave the countries in which they are born, without waiting until they return to the firm's country of origin; in other words, it should be the exit of profits, not the entry, which should activate taxation. An objection which might be made here is that tax havens may simply be used as points in transit, and the funds which leave one country can return to another; this facility could conceivably be advantageous to developing countries themselves. But this objection would be nullified at the same time as tax-free profits are eliminated in tax havens by taxes being assessed as funds leave the countries in which they have created profits— except where it can be proved that they have been reinvested without delay in another host country. In any case, it is important to reduce the temptation for firms to set up their head offices in tax havens in the hope of thus avoiding immediate or deferred taxation of their profits in the rest of the world. The answer is quite simple: it would be enough if the United States and the European Community—or even the community itself—would refuse to allow the establishment of MNEs directed from tax havens. No MNE would take the chance of losing out on markets worth far more than any dubious savings in taxes.

It is equally important to examine the influence of systems of taxation on the different forms taken by capital inflows. The advantage of immediate taxation of consolidated profits, with full deduction made for taxes paid elsewhere, is that firms can then choose the most appropriate form of transfer payment, whether it be made in the form of dividends, interest, or royalties. When a country of origin taxes only those profits made on its own territory, or when it defers taxation of outside profits, it encourages firms to lend rather than to participate: for they thus avoid a tax on profits in the host country added to withholding taxes on remittances; in fact they are encouraged to borrow in order to increase their deductible expenses. Thus host countries must insist that there be a certain relation between capital inflows and borrowing; but a precise ratio would be hard to define or impose. Measures which increase fiscal receipts are not necessarily those which are most appropriate in terms of avoiding either outside control or a greater burden on the balance of payments.

As for the effects on development: purely territorial taxation, as well as deferred taxation of outside profits up until the time they are repatriated, allows for the continued existence of disastrous competition between underdeveloped countries to attract MNEs by way of tax concessions. An agreement, however difficult to conceive, is indispensable to restrict these concessions, and submit them to objective criteria and time limits. These concessions can, at any rate, be partially cancelled by the way each country of origin taxes its own companies. A general convention, or several bilateral ones, would be called for, fixing the conditions under which countries of origin will allow their MNEs to benefit from fiscal concessions to be obtained in host countries without paying all the more at home. Once again it is a matter of general measures, which could be applied as easily to local enterprises as to foreign ones, and which would cater to the needs of regional development as well as regional balance. Similar measures would adjust the system of immediate taxation on overall profits. Another general agreement that would be required, of course, is one which would limit the advantages granted by developed countries to firms which invest in their economies—for the poorer countries cannot possibly offer such advantages without seriously increasing the inequities which already exist, that is, the tendency for the rich to get richer. An intelligent policy for aiding development would be one that defined the criteria according to which the more developed countries would accord fiscal concessions to their own firms to encourage the necessary investments in the underdeveloped world.

One could even imagine a kind of automatic aid. Assuming that the main industrialized countries opted for a system of immediate taxation of overall profits with deductions allowed for taxes paid abroad, it would not be more costly for firms to pay taxes preferably in the underdeveloped countries in which they operate. It would be enough to adopt the principle that in case of nationalization, the taxes paid on local profits would be one of the main elements to be taken into account in calculating compensation; or in calculating the amount which may be repatriated in case of the partial or total sale of a subsidiary. Insofar as firms have a certain flexibility as to the places where they have their profits appear, they would thus be encouraged to pay taxes voluntarily in the developing countries without any increase in their costs. Measures of this kind would make up for a tendency to reduce the aid so grudgingly given by governments, and accepted by legislatures. By the substance of their contributions as well as by the security they would create, they would also improve markedly the relations between the MNEs and the countries in which they establish themselves.

TRANSFER PRICES

An international tax reform would eliminate one of the main factors responsible for distorting prices in the relations between branches of a group. This is a matter of interest to tax authorities in at least a few countries; the United States and West Germany are foremost in this field. The severity of their laws is such that it can lead even to double taxation. When the American tax authorities attribute part of headquarters' expenses to a firm's branches abroad, the profits taxed at home are thereby increased; if the host countries do not permit corresponding deductions, a fraction of the profits is thus taxed twice. The setting of prices between subsidiaries is no less a means of having profits appear where the risk is slight and taxation least heavy. Suppose an MNE operates in two countries—it would have a tendency to raise the price of sales made to a branch situated in the country where it wants to minimize profits and on the contrary, reduce prices to the other branch. A similar practice is possible between branches of a firm located in one country: unless local taxes represent a major part, the state will come out ahead. On the other hand, in the relations of branches of the same firm located in several countries, one country might lose, and another gain. A transfer of revenues and a transfer of taxation exist at the same time. It is true that the various administrations within one country can have contradictory interests: overestimated import prices will reduce taxable profits, while at the same time raising the customs revenue. The other difficulty is that tax authorities in different countries are lukewarm to cooperating with each other on this level. They have doubts about communicating documents reserved for the tax base—and some are afraid of losing unwarranted advantages to others.

With the internationalization of business, most of this sort of price manipulation renders meaningless all balance-of-payments statistics. When intracompany commerce represents a third of world commerce, it is difficult to understand the significance of a surplus or a deficit which can be profoundly influenced by the prices mutually charged by the affiliates of some of the larger groups. It came as a great surprise a few years ago that the United States, quite naturally, had a surplus balance of patents and licenses with all countries, and had a deficit in this regard only in its relations with Canada. It is a sure bet that the patents appeared in a country where corporation taxes were most favorable.

It would be wrong to say that this difficulty is to be found in all types of MNE. Those which use local resources for the local market—the food industry is largely of this type—only rarely make deliveries from one subsidiary to another. The same may be said for those which manufacture several models which differ from country to country and depend mainly on local resources for their manufacture. But this is not the case generally. The most typical sort of problem appears as soon as there is a degree of vertical integration, as in the oil industry, which goes from the oil wells to the gasoline pumps by way of transportation and refining. The most complete division of labor is the production of components in different places with a view to the lowest costs and their assembly in one of these places or in yet another one; then the price of supplies between subsidiaries has an obvious effect; and generally there is no MNE which will deprive itself of the greatest advantages of supplying capital, technology, and services to its members.

This is not a simple problem. National tax services try whenever possible to find a reference in the prices which would prevail between independent buyers and sellers of the same products or the same services. But in fact there is no such thing as a fair price for technology and many of the mechanical, electronic, or chemical components have no other purpose than the product itself which is created within the network of the firm. Moreover, there is no absolutely valid principle by which to divide the general operating costs of a firm among different subsidiaries; this is even less so for the costs of research, especially the more hazardous kind, that is, oil exploration; or research in the chemical or pharmaceutical industries where discoveries of therapeutic or commercially useable properties occur once in every 10,000 molecules subjected to synthesis.

Thus there is room for maneuver. The incentives for manipulating the costs of transactions between subsidiaries can be attributed to a variety of motives; which for the sake of analysis may be divided roughly according to internal and external factors.

Even if there were no fiscal disparity or risk differential, an MNE might find it to its advantage to show a profit either at the head office or at those subsidiaries where its participation is greatest, rather than in places where it would have to be shared with other partners. Nor is it out of the question that a group may show smaller profits in countries where the labor unions are most demanding.

The external factors might depend either on the clumsiness of one state or on disparities in the behavior of several. For instance, a country where the currency tends to appreciate would be the place where profits would be made to appear; the reverse would be true where there is a risk of depreciation. There is also no lack of countries applying different rules when it comes to exchange controls governing remittance abroad of various forms of payments and capital revenue. There is the example of the pharmaceutical company whose subsidiary in Colombia made very little profit, but which nevertheless paid to the head office high interests and large dues for patents. The fact was that there was a strict limit on the remittance of dividends, while transfers of funds abroad were more freely authorized for other forms of remuneration considered to be current transactions. Naturally, disparities in tax bases and tax rates, the facilities offered by tax havens, etc., provide plenty of opportunity for the wiliness of foreign investors.

It cannot be repeated often enough that before countries can blame MNEs they must review their own rules of behavior and introduce such corrections as they will later find inevitable—otherwise they should not be surprised when large profit-motivated firms take advantage of each opportunity and creep through every loophole. Among the changes which must be made are (1) the revision of exchange controls so that the same treatment will be given to all sorts of capital remittances abroad; (2) international tax reform in order to end once and for all the easy ways out offered by tax havens; (3) better still, the setting up of a system including immediate taxation of worldwide profits which would encourage all host countries to bring their tax rates into line with those of the industrialized countries; and (4) rectification of the price scales applied to transfers of goods and services between subsidiaries of the same firm, either by applying an objective reference, or by demanding of a group that its policy remain coherent on this score (for example, by calculating the prices of such transfers on a "cost plus" basis, but following a certain uniformity in its general practice everywhere.)

As for distortions of an internal character, they cannot be corrected without higher standards of disclosure on the part of the MNEs: that is to say, information on supplies and prices to be made available whatever the circumstances to anyone interested—partners, countries of origin, host countries, suppliers, customers, and workers. By its very existence, such publicity would have a moderating effect; it would make it possible, furthermore, to apply the principle of nondiscrimination as it is expressed in American legislation; namely, that a firm does not have the right, on pain of having to compensate those it discriminated against, to apply different prices for similar transactions with different customers, *unless* the difference can be justified by the volume and regularity of the supplies.

RESTRICTING OF MARKETS

The manipulation of prices between subsidiaries can constitute a hidden means of allocating markets among them or license holders of the same group. It would be enough, for example, to raise the cost of purchases applied to some of them to remove their competitiveness for exports. But the dividing of markets can be even more direct. The granting of licenses is often accompanied by export restrictions to avoid competition with the enterprise itself, or with its other license holders. In a large number of activities a de facto distribution can result from the very functioning of the group, from the guidelines given to its subsidiaries.

The group of experts commissioned by UNCTAD have made a report on restrictive practices. The subject was not limited to MNEs, but extended to the conditions which often accompany the use of patents, licenses, or brand names. The report noted that though there is an international organization for intellectual property, it is more often used to protect rights than to prevent abuse. Among the undesirable practices it named were export restrictions; tied sales—that is to say, where the buyer can only obtain a certain product if he agrees to buy other products; payments by buyers of licenses for techniques which are not indispensable to them; and even the license dues which extend far beyond the duration of the patents themselves. The experts tried to classify these practices according to the degree of damages they entail and to suggest compensatory advantages with which they might be combined to make them acceptable. But the report also expressed the wish that the same rules apply to the internal practices within a firm's network as to the relations created by the sale of technology between independent firms.

It is important, in this regard, to underline the special characteristics of an MNE and the difficulty in disentangling certain practices from the overall advantages they may bring. It has already been noted that there is a big difference between a group which must take care to avoid the losses which one subsidiary may cause another, and the independent firm which can afford to ignore the losses it provokes for others. In the opposite sense, transfer of technology can be inseparable from certain restrictions without which the owner of a process or product would not grant a license. The advantages of large-scale organization are more obvious within a group, where subsidiaries are 100 percent owned or are subject to majority control. In the case of minority participation, the agreement looks very much like a cartel. Yet prohibitions which appear quite natural today, which are typical of American legislation and which are growing in the European Community and in Japan as well, should not be allowed to be twisted in such a way as to have cartels simply replaced by large conglomerations.

This is not to say that this difficulty appears in all MNEs. Once again, those which use local resources to satisfy local demands know neither transfer prices nor market splitting, for they are involved in almost no exporting. There should be no confusion, however, between the splitting up of markets and specialization, whether the latter is in the shape of production of different components in different countries and the assembly of those components in one of them, or the production of different models destined for all the markets. Nor should this matter be confused with the creation of subsidiaries on the spot, banks or commercial houses, for example, to serve the local market. The difficulty is greatest for those groups which manufacture comparable and competitive products in different locations.

In order to encourage the establishment of an industry, a country might, to begin with, accept limitations on exports in competition with other subsidiaries in the same group; such a sacrifice might indeed be very small at the outset. Export capacity, after all, requires that a certain size be reached to lower cost prices sufficiently. Later, however, such a limitation might seem very heavy.

For such a restriction to be acceptable it must, therefore, be compensated for by lower prices on technology transfers and a time limit. The U.N. group on MNEs recommended that firms announce quite clearly, at the outset, which restrictions they would impose on their subsidiaries, what sort of justifications they would invoke, and for what period of time; after which conditions could be renegotiated.

Such a procedure is more easily applied to the future than to the past. However, when a regional union is being formed, the rules by which manufactures and outlets are distributed among member countries, are likely to become a serious obstacle to integration itself. The Common Market set an example by annulling certain exclusivity clauses. It should be acknowledged, moreover, that where a regional union is being formed, private export restrictions between member countries must, as a rule, be cancelled even if, in practice, this would appear to create some retroactivity. The widening of the market must be considered to be a sufficient compensation for such retroactive action.

An international agreement would be the most effective way of reinforcing the negotiating powers of the weaker countries. It would establish that, in principle, export restrictions are not a matter of right, unless it can be shown, by the group applying them, that they result in lower cost prices, that each of the countries involved received compensatory advantages and, moreover, that such a practice contributes to their overall advantage.

The home countries of firms can bring very precious assistance in such cases. The European Community already foresees the day when it will close its borders to products which are subject to market sharing practices contrary to its own principles. More generally, countries of origin (basically the community, the United States, and Japan) can agree that developing countries tie profit remittances to results obtained by the exports of the subsidiaries of MNEs. This would be a legitimate inducement to avoid unjustified restrictions, to increase the capacity of the host countries to acquire the necessary outside outlets, to permit the specialization of production and an intensification of exchange, instead of autarchic manufacturing entirely directed towards each separate market.

INTERNATIONAL REGULATION

United action is what is lacking today, yet it is absolutely necessary to regulate international concentrations; that is, where a firm in one country acquires an equity, control, or even total ownership of a firm in another country, or where two or more firms of different origins become associated to create a common subsidiary. One comes up against an extraordinary contradiction here. Either no action at all is possible—that which could be prevented in one country would not be preventable between countries—or one of the states concerned objects to the operation and in this way threatens to apply its jurisdiction extraterritorially with a resulting risk of conflict.

For a long time the United States was the only country to have real antitrust legislation. As winding as the course of the jurisprudence around it may have been, it was concerned only at first with effects on internal competition. This is one of the maladjustments which caused firms, thwarted from within, to make acquisitions abroad. While on account of their size they were enjoined not to buy up other American firms engaged in the same lines of activity, nothing prevented them from making such acquisitions among firms located outside of the United States. American jurisprudence has been modified, to the extent, in fact, where it has prevented Gillette from buying up a German manufacturer of electric shavers. Such a measure was perhaps perfectly justifiable, but the fact remains that the United States made a decision in a matter which was equally within the province of the Federal German Republic.

It must also be realized that the American antitrust legislation has not only been used to maintain competition. It has been deflected from its objective and has, on the contrary, been used to diminish the competitive capacity of outside firms. This was the case, for instance, in Canada, when it blocked the merger of two subsidiaries of separate American firms, an action which prevented them from becoming big enough to constitute a threat to other Canadian firms or to the American market. In the same way the Renault-Peugeot agreement to sell their cars jointly on the American market was blocked, though the arrangement had been blessed and even encouraged by the French government. Since their total sales would have represented only a small fraction of the American automobile market this kind of purism is, in fact, equivalent to a misappropriation of power; far from maintaining effective competition, it protects vested interests.

Europe has begun to set up its own policy on competition. So far whatever action has been taken has been taken by each state separately and has given rise to much ambivalence: on the one hand, the tendency of certain bodies to favor regroupings with the conviction that a greater size reinforces firms; and on the other, the efforts of other organisms in the same country concerned with preventing the formation of monopolies. Much of the rejection of large groupings has been directed against takeovers by foreign firms. There is no control on a European scale except for those firms depending on the European Coal and Steel Community. But the Commission of the European Community has begun to elaborate some proposals. These would be directed only against large-size concentrations involving $1 billion of sales per year or more. Japan, for its part, has a Monopolies Commission; but as was revealed when the two largest iron smelting firms proposed a merger, it only has the power of delaying action.

Undoubtedly the best solution would be an international agreement, but this is not about to be enacted. In the meantime one cannot ask of a country that it remain indifferent to such operations as are of concern to it, just because they might have international repercussions. The best that can be suggested is that in cases where a foreign enterprise is implicated, measures taken unilaterally by a government be applied temporarily and that a final decision be put off until the other government has been fully consulted.

International regulation would demand at least an agreement on the criteria and the procedures between the main countries of origin which means in fact Japan, the United States, the European Community and its associates. The problem is that the American procedure is no more acceptable to the Europeans than that envisaged by the community would be to the United States. The American procedure consists of intervention after the fact without any prior warning. If a firm seems to be attaining monopoly status, it can be forced to get rid of some of its subsidiaries or withdraw some of its participation. The European Community's Commission proposes a procedure requiring prior authorization for very large groupings with the possibility of suspending the operation for a maximum of nine months. Uncertainty of this kind could play havoc with the shares of the firms involved and even upset the stock exchange as a whole. Something better will have to be devised!

An original type of agreement could be envisaged which would avoid the inconvenient aspects of both the American procedure and the European project. The first rule must be that all grouping operations be made publicly, in other words, that all secret purchases on the stock market be banished; in fact, these allow for no supervision and they perturb the market as well; the only two acceptable procedures would be direct negotiation or a takeover bid. The second rule would be that operations of this order be announced to the competent regulating body.

This announcement would be accompanied by a declaration of the objectives being pursued: these must include more than the simple goal of eliminating competition or increasing profits; there must also be aims of general interest such as rationalization of operations, extension of production, the development of exports or research, the creation of jobs, or the improvement of working conditions. The operation could proceed without delay, but its effects would be watched and compared to the objectives of general interest declared at the outset. If the operation were found wanting in this respect, it could be dissolved.

A harmonization of this kind among the larger countries of origin would allow contradictions to be eliminated; and a full consultation with the interested states would bring to bear the power of the bigger countries on behalf of the poorer developing ones.

LABOR RELATIONS

The labor relations field is one in which there might appear to be a conflict of interests between the workers of a home country and those of a host country. Labor unions tend to consider the fact that lower wages are paid in other countries as unfair competition. This is an obvious oversimplification. How is a poor country to pay wages comparable to those paid in the United States? The low rate of income reflects low productivity. Production costs can thus be higher despite remarkably low wages. It is not even enough to consider the labor cost per unit produced, that is to say, the hourly rate plus extra expenses divided by the number of products per hour. The other production costs can also be heavier, if for example the scale of production remains too small, if equipment imported from far away is more expensive, if transportation or energy costs are especially high.

In the face of this widespread attitude on the part of labor unions in the developed countries, the governments of underdeveloped countries and often the workers themselves point out that low labor costs are about their only valid resource, and that any measures taken to raise labor costs artificially would at the same time destroy job opportunities as well as their competitive capacity and chances for development.

As a matter of fact employment is the very heart of the Third World's predicament, and the MNEs cannot provide the answer on a sufficiently large scale. We have already seen the necessity of keeping a certain number of people more productively employed on the land, people who would otherwise fill the shantytowns and swell open or concealed unemployment. This should not mean that the developing countries are forever condemned to restricting themselves to the simplest industrial employment, while the workers of the industrialized world enjoy the more sophisticated and highly paid jobs. Some developing countries already have begun to work with advanced techniques. But there is a division of labor from the start; and what is most important is that nothing be put in the way of the creation of jobs which correspond to the capacities of the Third World's labor force.

The most acute difficulty appears, nevertheless, when into a generally backward economic setting MNEs introduce their technology, even when this is not the most advanced. Modern production techniques combined with low wage levels add up to an unbeatable competitiveness. Protectionist reactions in the industrialized countries can only be avoided if the transfer of activity is sufficiently gradual, full employment is generally guaranteed, and reemployment assistance is sufficiently generous.

But this gap causes many problems for the developing countries themselves. One of these is that the firm whose productivity is far superior to the national average will offer wages far higher than current rates. Thus there is a chance that a kind of enclave will be created and that other activities will not be able to develop in the face of such wage levels. In other words a dislocation of the labor market will result which will only be another obstacle to the diffusion of progress.

On the other hand, firms may pay wages at current rates and thus avoid such dislocation, in which case their profits are likely to grow considerably. If these firms work only for an internal market, price controls are conceivable which, by reducing their margins, would be a means of raising the real incomes of the population. But such a method is not easily compatible with international commerce. Insofar as a country has an efficient system of taxation of profits, or a well-adjusted social security scheme, the capacity to pay higher wages will be absorbed by taxes or dues; and the host country will receive the means of spreading the benefits of this isolated productivity over larger segments of the population. In other words, the effects of development would be diffused and inequalities would be corrected. Failing the existence of such general means, a solution could be found in the establishment of a social fund into which could be paid remunerations in excess of the usual rates to which the firm in question is invited to conform. Experience shows that such a locking device is more worthwhile than allowing serious wage disparities to arise, and by the effect of example letting the highest ones become general.

Another objection to which an answer must be found is the weakening of the unions' powers of negotiation in the face of MNEs. Decisions may swing between the local executives and the firm's headquarters, and union organizers often have the impression that they are being sent from one to the other. To this is added a possible threat, if not to close down, at least not to develop an establishment in a place where labor makes strong demands. The unions also dread that even a strike can be broken when there are other subsidiaries which will supply parts to take the place of interrupted production.

A first answer where wage negotiations are concerned would be full delegation of all powers in this domain to the local management. If, however, centralized decisions are involved, the unions in all countries concerned must be enabled to negotiate collectively with the company's headquarters.

Unions want to feel free to use their solidarity to counterbalance the great power of the MNEs. Certain countries, however, forbid this kind of strike, either by law or through jurisprudence, even though they are not more frequent in the more liberal countries which are not particularly opposed to them. Yet such movements can entail unbearably heavy costs, especially for workers in developing countries; they may in some cases be contrary to wage agreements signed for several years to come. In such cases, the only counterbalance left is government action against strike-breaking deliveries from other subsidiaries.

The Diffusion of Progress

Protests against abnormal conditions come into their own again not when they are aimed at the low level of wages, where it is justified by the level of underdevelopment; but rather against the establishment of MNEs and the development of their production in locations where safety and hygiene standards are less severe, and more generally when the level of wages is not a result of free negotiations but rather of repressive and discriminatory regimes. Unions feel quite legitimately that MNEs should publish the conditions of work and job security by which they will abide, or which are in effect in their countries of origin; and that these should be relaxed only with the agreement of the host country and the workers' representatives.

The Havana Charter which was to establish a world trade organization, but which was never ratified, already expressed certain doubts about labor relations and the establishment of wages. The underlying idea was that the most-favored-nation clause, by eliminating discrimination, would lead to a better distribution of resources only if wages were established freely at a level commensurate with productivity while paying due regard to other costs. This will not happen by itself, especially not when all collective bargaining is prohibited, all strike attempts are repressed by severest sanctions, including imprisonment and intervention by the police or armed forces who scarcely hesitate before opening fire. Nor is a balance more easily established in countries which practice racial discrimination. No doubt the economists who favor free trade will say that consumers will benefit from lower prices. But the producers have the right to another conception of the division of labor, to reject abnormal competition. The GATT agreement which was put into operation when the Havana Charter failed to be ratified, asked that the contracting parties respect the charter. Thus a recognized means for combatting repressive or discriminatory regimes would be to refuse them the benefit of the most-favored-nation clause; they would become eligible for it only when they can show that wage levels in their country are being established in a manner that is in proportion to productivity and progress.

It goes without saying that the difficulty is all the more serious as MNEs increase their competitive advantages by grafting their technical advances onto a wage base kept artificially low by repression and discrimination. In South Africa certain MNEs much in demand have stipulated that, national legislation notwithstanding, they be allowed to pay the same wages to white and black workers. These MNEs won their case.

The governments of home countries would gain much distinction, they would respond to the legitimate preoccupations of their labor force, and they would contribute to the general spreading of a respect for human working conditions if they took the means of preventing their firms from establishing themselves in countries which do not abide by these principles. At least they could make their grants of authorization dependent upon firms getting undertakings from host countries as to their being allowed to respect human rights. There is no lack of means to this end. Countries which offer guarantees to their firms for their investments abroad, can refuse the benefits of this insurance to those which contravene these rules. The countries of origin could also threaten to refuse access to their products: from then on those firms which would profit from abnormal facilities would have to satisfy themselves with local markets, with no chances of exporting. Another technique would be the refusal of any deduction for any taxes which might have been paid in those host countries which do not respect certain recognized international principles.

Whether or not MNEs become instruments for the creation of a more humane society depends, in the last analysis, on enlightened action by the home countries.

Two U.N. documents prepared for the conference on raw materials and development held in New York City in April 1974 have drawn a spectacular picture of the situation in the Third World; using 1970 trade statistics and 1974 prices, they manage to illustrate with breathtaking clarity the divergent situations and abrupt reversals to be found there.

In 1970, oil and its derivatives alone absorbed 30 percent of world trade, of all commodities, copper absorbed 7 percent, and wheat and coffee combined, scarcely more. Contrary to what might be supposed, developing countries supplied only 38 percent of these world exports, though they then represented three-fourths of their own sales. The industrialized countries with market economies exported 55 percent of the total, while they depended on it for only 25 percent of their export trade.

In only one-third of all commodities is the developing world's share of exports more than half. Fifty percent of the Third World's commodity exports are made up of oil. To find the next quarter one must add together all exports of coffee, sugar, and cotton. On the import side, the Third World represents only one-sixth of world trade, one-fifth for manufactured products, one-eighth for commodities; and, once again, oil, wheat and rice represent half of its primary imports.

If one were to compare exports and imports for the Third World as a whole, one would discover a surplus of $25 billion on primary products, which compensates exactly for the deficit on manufactured products. However, to mix facts together in this way doesn't make sense. On the one hand, there is already the $8 billion surplus of the oil producers, which represents 40 percent of their export figures; the $1.5 billion surplus of the producers of metal ores which account for 30 percent of their sales figures; while the rest of the Third World countries have a

96

deficit of $10 billion on commodities themselves, that is, 35 percent of their imports of these products.

AN ABRUPT REVERSAL

At this point one becomes aware of a spectacular shift. In fact, only approximate estimates exist so far of the upheaval of world trade that has been caused by radical price fluctuations. Manufactured products continue to rise with inflation, while oil quintuples and zinc and phosphates have almost quadrupled. At the other end of the scale, some primary products go up less than manufactured products; tea and jute are typical examples, and all the sadder in that they are the principal exports of India and Pakistan, two of the largest and poorest countries in the world.

The U.N. document provides only a temporary evaluation as it confined itself to trade figures generally known, those for 1970, and applied to them prices of the end of 1973 and beginning of 1974. Yet they manage to show world exports doubling. At the same time, they indicate two upheavals: commodity exports have increased in value by more than 180 percent; those of manufactured products, even allowing for a rise of 10 percent in 1974, did not appreciate by more than 55 percent. The share of commodities in world trade thus leapt from 35 percent to 55 percent. Exports of oil products, instead of $24 billion, were worth $135 billion; instead of accounting for less than 8 percent of world exports, they now represent 23 percent—and 45 percent of total commodities.

The developing countries' share of commodity exports goes from 38 percent to 48 percent; that of industrialized countries falls from 55 percent to 45 percent—the subsequent decline in the price of wheat, exported for the most part by industrialized countries, probably diminished their part somewhat further. In total world trade, the developing countries see their share growing from 17 percent to 27 percent, but oil—instead of 33 percent—now accounts for 62 percent of their exports. At the same time, unfortunately, it rises from 7 percent to 22 percent in their imports.

The rise in price of certain products, the stagnation of others, the shifts in exporter or importer positions have given rise to unbelievable divergencies within the Third World. Nothing is as misleading as the old idea which confused the variation in the price ratio between raw materials and manufactured products with the relations between underdeveloped and developed countries. One must not forget that the industrialized countries are themselves large exporters of raw materials: for some time the biggest decreases occurred in the price of cereals other than rice, that is, those for which the industrialized countries are the main suppliers.

Today the problem of import prices versus export prices, in other words the terms of trade, has a profound effect on the industrialized countries themselves; it is, however, above all between the Third World countries that a gulf is being created: some are getting richer and others poorer through the very new relationship among themselves.

TRENDS

Quite clearly, it becomes more irrelevant than ever to think of and treat the Third World as a bloc. Here are the developed countries, who had been used to financing quite easily with other revenue their $8 billion trade deficit, suddenly confronted with a tenfold increase: an $80 billion trade deficit, representing 18 percent of their imports as against 3.6 percent before. Even though their surplus on the sales of manufactured goods increased by 55 percent, their deficit on commodities was multiplied by three and a half. Taken individually, they now contemplate a trade deficit spread between $5 and $15 billion; the all-time enormous record previously held by the United States alone had been only $7 billion.

Where developing countries are concerned, the surplus is an overall $60 billion, or 60 percent of their import figures, 37 percent of their exports. But, again, this kind of overall view is deceptive. The oil producing countries' surplus leaps from $8 billion to a prodigious $78 billion, that is to say, from 43 percent to 78 percent of their sales; among the others one notes a 70 percent increase in the surplus on commodities; but, on the contrary, the countries which do not share this good fortune watch their deficits climb by $10 billion, a charge which is added to the existing deficit on manufactured products: that is to say, $22 billion—on the whole —as against $10 billion previously, 36 percent of their imports as against the 30 percent which they had previously been able to meet only with the greatest difficulty.

Nor can one ignore changes in quantity: some, like those of metals, have not stopped increasing. Others are more sensitive to variations in prices. And in those areas where the prices of raw materials show the least rise, it is simply a result of decreased demand. In terms of value, the inequalities are even greater than one would be led to believe by simply applying price rises to 1970 trade figures. The Third World can be divided into three parts: (1) the countries which have so much money that they do not know what to do with it; (2) those for whom price increases in other raw materials have allowed them to meet the higher oil prices; and (3) those who are the all-time losers, because they now have to pay more for oil and other raw materials as well—the prices of the manufactured goods they import have gone up too, although somewhat less, but in any case, that which they have to sell has increased far less than that which they have to import.

When one looks at the evolution of prices over a longer period, one fact stands out. Raw materials do not get back up to their 1950 index until 1970; during this period manufactured goods have risen by 25 percent in the first ten years and by 10 percent in the second decade. This would seem to support the theory that in the long run price relationships tend to change to the disadvantage of raw materials producers. But from 1970 on, and particularly in 1972, the reversal is quite abrupt. All raw materials go up in price; there are only a few exceptions, bauxite and aluminum, tea and jute. The average price rise is 100 percent, three-fifths of it taking place from 1973 on. The recovery in the terms of trade is fantastic, rising by some 45 percent. A number of factors can be singled out to help explain this movement. There is suddenly a shortage of wheat after huge surpluses, but the most spectacular rise is in the price of beef. An excessive increase in energy consumption now provides the oil producers with fertile ground for concerted action, as was demonstrated at the time of the Yom Kippur War. And, more generally, for what is almost the first time the industrialized world finds itself in the midst of a period of both expansion and inflation. The speculation on gold betrays not only fears about the future of currencies, but the disintegration of the monetary system itself.

All these reversals and upheavals should discourage economic theories which would make a structural characteristic of the relationship between the prices of raw materials and of manufactured goods. In fact, there has been a remarkable reversal in doctrine.

The founders of classic economic theory considered that increases in the price of natural resources were inevitable and that they would continue to the detriment of both wages and profits. Intellectual fashions since the 1940s suggested that, on the contrary, raw materials would continue to decline in comparison with industrial products; in a word, the developing countries which depend on raw materials exports would only become poorer as they received relatively lower prices for them while at the same time paying even higher prices for their imports of industrial products. Though they may seem to be so, these two theses are not contradictory; the classical and modern economists were, in fact, not dealing with the same problem.

Ricardo's theory of the rent is a familiar one. He emphasized that as production increased it would extend to less and less fertile lands. Food prices would thus have to cover rising costs while the better situated producers got the benefits of a "free ride." Hence the view of an evolutionary process whereby natural resources absorb an ever larger part of incomes, to the disadvantage of both capitalists and workers.

This law of diminishing returns may apply where there is a question of land use, in land which is known; it can also be extended to the development of hydroelectric power sites. When it is a matter of resources extracted from the earth, accidental discoveries make a mockery of predictions. The richest South African gold mines were discovered long after those of the United States, Arabian oil long after Pennsylvania's, the mountains of iron in Africa and Brazil long after the "minette" of Lorraine. Furthermore, extraction technology is undergoing radical changes: the first coal was withdrawn in buckets at the end of a rope; today strip mining in the United States is done with bulldozers. Thus the cost of raw materials follows no general law. Nonetheless, the rise in the prices of land, a nonextensible resource, along with the increase in the mass of capital and the productivity of labor, revives the classical theory.

The opposite argument was based on both production structures and those of demand. This is Prebisch's famous thesis: As incomes go up, food consumption absorbs a diminishing part of demand; as for raw materials, as the degree of manufacturing and service costs increases, the relation of raw materials to overall production becomes less and less important. The most original aspect of this thesis, but also the most controversial, is that raw materials emanate from producers in competition with each other, while the manufacturing industry operates as a monopoly. When productivity among the former goes up, prices go down. Among the latter group, workers and employers act in collusion to keep wages and profits climbing.

The first question one must ask is whether this picture is true to life. It is a fact that certain agricultural products like cocoa, coffee, sugar, and even peanuts (aside from those produced by some industrial firms which incidentally failed in both French and British Africa) are produced on very small farms. On the other hand, heavier raw materials and sources of energy are, for the most part, exploited by enormous MNEs. It is hard, therefore, to derive from the contrast of "monopolies versus competition," a structural origin of long-term differences in price movements.

Again the scene changes. Many studies, the most impressive of which is that of the Club of Rome, speak of the gradual exhaustion of raw materials as their exploitation is intensified to keep up with industrial growth. Questions are being asked about what will be left by the end of the century. Calculations are being made about the increased cost of extracting ever lower-grade minerals, and even of the possibility of extracting aluminum from clay and titanium from seawater. It goes without saying that in this apocalyptic view of the future, raw materials for industry as well as energy sources will benefit from scarcity values of increasing proportions. This would extend even to food products unless the Green Revolution changes the outlook, since world production would not be able to keep pace with growing populations.

All this needs to be examined more closely. Any comparison between trends or the difference of two indices depends entirely on what points of departure are used. It goes without saying that if raw material prices are being considered at a moment when a worldwide scarcity is sending them sky high, for example, at the time of the Korean War, a renewal of comparable market tension will be needed before the primary producers' position again appears as favored. The reverse was the case, for instance, during the second decade between the two world wars: the primary products market had collapsed under the impact of the world crisis. Never again were market conditions to be as bad for primary products. Thus it is difficult to distinguish a long-term tendency—and the most profound statistical analysis will confirm this. At the same time, to expect today that prices will continue to rise ever more sharply would be to jump to the conclusion that fluctuations have come to an end.

The strangest thing about the discussion that is in full swing on this question is that it is taking place in the absence of any yardstick against which international price movements might be measured. The usual calculations of the terms of trade are based on the indices of unit export and import values published by various countries and often themselves computed by differing methods. One would really have to know how these various figures are arrived at. Averages are usually calculated by categorizing products and dividing overall values by physical units, that is, numbers or tonnage. The National Bureau of Economic Research sponsored a pilot study on international prices which was done by Irving Kravis. In it the author showed up the errors inherent in this method. A difference in overall values can just as well result from a change in the composition of a class of products as from a change in prices. At its worst, a lowering of average values can even result from a rise in prices. For example, a country which places automobiles and spare parts in the same category may, for some reason or other, virtually price itself out of the car market and find itself selling only parts: the sum of receipts divided by tonnage will thus move in the opposite direction from that of car prices.

There are only two countries in the world which, in addition to unit values, calculate import and export price indices as well; these are Germany and Japan. Like those used for internal prices, such indices adhere to a fixed base for a number of years; they gather a constant basket of products, for sales as well as for purchases. A comparison of these indices with those of unit values shows up profound divergencies. Yet, even import and export price indices are poor indicators of relative trends or of the favorable or unfavorable external trade position of a country. The composition of trade is, after all, in each case that of a particular country; prices are, therefore, weighted by the categories established for its own sales and purchases. A more significant index would have an international weighting included in its calculation; that is, it would take into account the relative weight of each type of product in world trade as a whole. Only in this way could significant conclusions be reached.

INDUSTRIAL PRICES

If one looks at price trends within the most advanced economies, one finds that they are most stable at the level of industrial production. Nonetheless, even though industrial prices used to vary little, the general inflationary tendency remained—caused by agricultural policies, rent increases, and the upward tendency in the price of services. Within the European framework, the more optimistic hypotheses were predicated on absolute price stability in industrial production; even so, estimates revealed that one would not be able to escape from a general price increase of about 2.5 percent per year. In the years 1960-66, when the United States managed to combine a high rate of expansion with almost absolute price stability, it was able to do so only by compensating for other increases by a gradual lowering of industrial prices.

In international trade, industrial prices have long been even more stable. The OECD report on inflation noted that it was only through exceptional circumstances from 1967 on that a price rise in this area was triggered off. Even so, in spite of continuing inflation throughout the world, the movement of industrial export prices has tended to slow down. The former acceleration could be attributed to the revaluation of the deutsche mark; the considerable weight of the German Federal Republic on the international industrial products market makes it a sort of price leader. Besides, in this case, a revaluation does not produce, as one might expect, a leveling off of internal prices; for the competitors tend to follow price rises instead of trying to block them. In more normal conditions, the effects are quite different: international competition tends to reduce price differences between producers of different countries and thus to maintain a general stability; provided, of course, it does not coincide, as has been the case in the 1970s, with rapid increases in the cost of basic supplies. It is easier in the light of this to understand the mechanism through which internal price trends influence each country's balance of trade. If a country sells less and thus incurs a growing deficit, it is not simply because its prices are higher; competition would not allow it. It is that the range of industries or firms which can still make a profit at international prices gets narrower and narrower as internal costs go up. The example of the United States before the devaluation of the dollar was very enlightening in this respect. One must, of course, set aside the sectors in which America maintains a kind of monopoly, the aerospace industry, nuclear energy, computer technology and advanced electronics. In the more traditional sectors, however, the United States had progressively been losing markets to its Japanese and German competitors. This was the case, for instance, for automobiles, machinery, or the chemical industry. This progressive shrinkage of external markets is simply a result of a shrinking area within which prices set by international competition still cover internal costs.

Thus it is not so much in the price ratio between raw materials and manufactured products, as within the primary sector itself that the clues to this difficulty will be found. Nevertheless, it is more a question of rapid fluctuations over a short time span, than of long-term trends. Apart from the fact that there is a blatant absence of solid statistical evidence on prolonged tendencies, there are two other comments to be made. First, one is too often inclined to assume that a lowering of price necessarily entails a lowering of profit; some sectors may benefit from improvements in productivity so rapid as to make price decreases almost inevitable, without altering profitability in any way. This was the case, for example, in the industrial sector between the time when aluminum was first produced and when production was developed on a large scale. In the same way changes in volume and production techniques brought about a rapid decline in domestic refrigerator prices. Second, in other respects, however sketchy the conclusions one may draw from unit value figures, the tables which GATT publishes regularly show that until 1971 lower price trends were less dominant in the field of primary products as a whole than in foodstuffs in particular. Moreover, they indicate that the price decrease mainly concerned cereals, and that except in the case of rice, industrialized countries were much more affected than the others. It is, in fact, in the area of cereals production that progress in yields has been most spectacular, to such an extent that cereals are still the most profitable of all agricultural produce.

We can, today, look at the recent past and at the same time ask ourselves questions about the future. Suddenly it is the industrialized countries, with the exception of the Federal German Republic, which have the largest deficits. The developing countries are divided—some are benefiting to the hilt from the price rises, while others bear the full brunt of them. What will happen next? So far the U.N. experts do not dare commit themselves, whereas those at the World Bank predict that the skyrocketing prices will prove to have been no more than a periodic difficulty and that, except for oil, most raw materials will fall as quickly as they have risen. Some good harvests will be all that is needed to bring down cereal prices; a slowdown in growth is bound to affect minerals;

automobile production has a direct effect on rubber prices; and the competition from synthetic fibers will continue to drive down the prices of natural fibers; this trend has in fact been interrupted by a short comeback of wool, while jute has been displaced by plastics and paper. The fact remains that the world has been guilty of an incredible lack of awareness, a scandalous inertia. Even before the spectacular reversals, fluctuations on primary products had continuously been explosive. It is already twenty-five years since a U.N. working group in 1950 tried to propose methods of stabilization, at least for compensation when the export revenue of a developing country collapsed, since the volumes and prices of its sales usually fall simultaneously. All that this has given rise to is a special fund of the IMF which allows for interest-bearing loans of a maximum duration of five years; according to the experts of this organization, historical experience shows that such a period is enough in all cases, for the trends governing any product to return to normal.

STABILIZATION SCHEMES

However, as we have now reached the stage where palliatives are no longer enough, why has the United States consistently been opposed to all price stabilization agreements? Does it consider it essential to its standard of living and growth to be able to obtain raw materials cheaply and to be able to take advantage of periods of low prices? Yet as a proportion of the total cost of national production, raw materials, except for food products, accounted for only 2 percent in the United States, 4 percent or 5 percent in Europe, and 7 percent in Japan. Considering what has happened since, the collective advantage of an economy is surely to accept prices that don't fall too low, particularly if such falls must soon thereafter be paid for by rises just as rapid. There is a big difference between the interests of a national economy and those of firms specialized in the raw materials trade, and which stand to make even bigger profits as they buy cheaply and sell when prices are on the upswing. The only valid objection to stabilizing mechanisms is that it is always difficult to distinguish between a fluctuation and a long-term trend; how can one tell if a fall in prices will be prolonged? The gradual sinking of the wool market seemed well established; there was ample reason for it since synthetic materials were continuously reducing demand for it; and yet the price of wool suddenly doubled—only to fall off once again.

Even while perfect methods of forecasting are lacking, difficulties need not be insurmountable; well-adjusted mechanisms could nonetheless be set up. The experts who had suggested financial compensation for a falling off of export revenues considered that a yearly guarantee should cover 95 percent of the receipts of the previous year; thus, if a trend were confirmed, the more serious repercussions would be largely avoided, while leaving room for the longer term adaptations that might have to be made.

To get back to basics, if expansion and inflation cause general upheavals, the fact remains that price movements of different products vary greatly in amplitude, and in less extreme circumstances price rises and falls can occur at the same time. Given a situation in which the developing countries produce something like half of the world's primary products (which represent for them three-fourths of their exports) there can be no continuing development, there can be no such thing as reasonable planning unless these basic instabilities are first attacked; that is to say, that the causes be recognized, that general measures be found to cope with them, and that inevitable complementary steps for certain products be developed.

DIVERGENCIES AMONG PRIMARY PRODUCTS

A better understanding of the divergencies in fluctuations affecting different types of products can be obtained on the basis of a working hypothesis; one which, by combining different aspects, would explain the variable behavior of markets.

This analysis would begin by classifying primary products according to three pairs of criteria. First, as to whether products are agricultural or nonagricultural—because one must set aside produce of the soil, the supply of which can be altered drastically by unforeseeable weather conditions. Nonagricultural products are not, of course, entirely immune to accidents either—their production may also, at times, be subject to sharp decreases, but the causes are usually political in nature.

Second, one must look at whether one is dealing with food products or with products intended for industrial use. This is an important distinction for explaining differences in the rate of worldwide demand. While the demand for raw materials in general may be affected by changes in industrial production in the major countries, it is, in fact, much more stable where food products are concerned.

The third element in this analysis is whether the products exported by primary producers constitute the main supply of the industrialized importers, or are the latter themselves producers who thus import only enough to complete their demand? Marginal products are subject to even greater fluctuations than others.

TABLE 2

Coffee and Cocoa: Prices and Production
(in U.S. cents per pound and thousands of metric tons)

Product and Producer	1970	1971	1972	1973	November 1973	March 1974
Coffee						
Brazil	53.94	45.17	50.74	66.53	71.25	73.37
Uganda	41.76	42.75	44.95	50.00	53.08	63.22
World	4,054	3,767	4,507	4,478	—	—
Latin America	2,426	2,104	2,890	2,837	—	—
Africa	1,314	1,276	1,304	1,300	—	April 1974
Cocoa						
Ghana	33.26	25.64	30.55	59.91	61.56	105.59
World	1,423	1,500	1,588	1,458	—	—
Latin America	387	352	373	362	—	—
Africa	1,000	1,105	1,170	1,051	—	—

Note: Coffee prices are at New York, cocoa prices, London. Dashes indicate figures not available.

Sources: Food and Agriculture Organization, *Commodity Review and Outlook*, 1972-1973, International Monetary Fund, *International Financial Statistics*, monthly.

By using these criteria one may begin to understand how the market behavior of each product can depend on the particular role it plays within this scheme. Cotton, for instance, is agricultural, though not a foodstuff, and is marginal to American needs in that the United States is itself a producer. The influence of each of these elements can be shown by very simple comparisons—and it requires comment.

Where food products are concerned, variations in overall supply can have a decisive effect. The rapid fluctuations in the price of wheat can be explained by a series of simultaneous droughts followed by better harvest prospects. In the case of beef, the almost permanent rise in prices is due to a perennial inability on the part of production to keep up with increasing demand. The rise in this area is steeper than in that of any primary product, steeper even than that of oil. But the export market of meat, like that of wheat, is marginal compared to the overall consumption. A better example of the effects of supply would be found in the cocoa market, where there are few producers, where the principal consumers import all the cocoa they use, and where the variations in price are almost entirely a consequence of production. The coffee market would be analogous, except that it is complicated by the competition between two different qualities and two different origins. African coffee has generally been less highly regarded than Latin American coffee; a difference in quality continues to persist; however, as the use of instant coffee becomes more widespread, more use will be made of the African varieties and the gap will gradually be filled. Table 2 summarizes these behavioral aspects in some characteristic markets.

Amplified Instability

The marginal character of certain imports can exaggerate their instability in terms of price as well as in terms of volume. Insofar as imports are only a supplement to basic supplies drawn from internal resources, all variations fall upon those imports. To illustrate this idea, let us suppose that on a given product purchases abroad represent 5 percent of total supply; if total demand varied by 5 percent in one direction or the other, imports could be either doubled or cancelled altogether. Untenable as it is, this is precisely the situation in which primary producers find themselves.

Where agricultural products are concerned, protectionist policies everywhere manage to exaggerate world market fluctuations.

There is worse to come. The methods of disposing of surpluses can further increase price and even market instability. The most explicit

TABLE 3

Selected Products: Wholesale Prices on the Relevant Markets
(cents)

Product and Producer	1969	1970	1971	1972	1973	1974	1975			
							January	February	March	April
Wheat (bushel)										
U.S.: Kansas City	1.39	1.48	1.58	1.84	3.58	4.68	4.30	4.11	3.76	3.64
Beef (100 pounds)										
U.S.: New York	38.93	41.32	42.51	49.76	63.67	53.19	37.88	42.22	41.67	45.90
Argentina: London	36.98	80.76	98.08	109.63	143.43	175.89 (April–June) 158.87 (July–September)	—	—	—	—
Sugar (100 pounds)										
Caribbean: New York	3.38	3.76	4.52	7.52	9.65	30.25	38.47	33.35	26.53	24.21
Cotton (100 pounds)										
U.S.: 12 markets	25.40	25.10	27.70	34.40	56.10	57.90	40.50	39.10	40.30	39.50
Egypt: Liverpool	63.20	62.60	61.72	65.29	74.15	153.61	136.90	138.00	—	—
Wool (100 pounds)										
Australia: Sydney	49.5	40.0	33.4	60.8	137.8	91.3	79.90	82.90	81.70	—
U.S.: Boston	45.8	46.6	35.1	48.8	85.0	63.1	41.80	41.00	41.00	—
Burlap (100 yards)										
India: New York	15.10	15.50	18.10	20.60	19.40	26.8	24.00	24.10	23.80	21.10

Note: Prices are at city noted. Dashes indicate data not available.

Source: IMF, *International Financial Statistics,* monthly.

example of this is that of sugar. The main part of sugar consumption in the European Community, as well as in the United States, is derived from the sugar beet. In addition each grants privileged import quotas at guaranteed prices to certain countries, the United States to Latin America, Europe to some of its dependent or associated territories abroad. On top of this arrangement, the community guarantees its own producers a minimum price up to a total volume slightly in excess of estimated consumption; it grants them a somewhat lower price for certain surplus quantities, and beyond that leaves them to find outlets at whatever price they can get. In these circumstances, it is not surprising that price fluctuations on the world sugar market should be more exaggerated than for any other product (see Table 3).

There is no denying either that those who have policies of selling off surpluses at any price are largely responsible for subsequent shortages. When the United States, but even more so the European Community, liquidated their wheat at prices far below the guaranteed domestic price, they proportionately reduced other countries' incentives to produce. Of course, the drought which hit certain parts of the Soviet Union and India at the same time, and which lasted for so long in the Sahel, was the major factor in the imbalance. But on top of this, production was discouraged in those regions which had the greatest need.

So dramatic an accident leads to an obvious recipe for action. It is high time that the principal producer countries of the temperate zones agreed to end their own export subsidies. Such practices have shown themselves to be disastrous. They involve heavy economic losses; disposing of surpluses at low prices, and then not having stocks available when demand goes into its upswing and could absorb a flow of goods at higher prices, is surely the height of improvidence. But on a human level it is all the more scandalous! Having hawked its goods at low prices, the world found itself without resources just as the threat of famine dawned— at a moment when these very goods might have served to save the lives of tens or hundreds of thousands of people. Yet, to renounce dumping altogether would have other important consequences. Each major producer would have to pay more attention to keeping its various prices in balance to avoid surpluses and shortages developing side by side. In the case of food surpluses the only solution, aside from foreign aid, would be stock-piling to provide in case of dearth or drought. This is to say that domestic production could remain stable without having such serious destabilizing effects on production abroad, and the difference between internal prices and world prices could finally be narrowed. The mere thought of the burden placed on the poorer countries by sudden price rises in the food they buy from the industrialized world is enough to demonstrate how important such an adjustment is. It would not only bring some order to agricultural policies, it would also eliminate a major obstacle, not only to development, but to survival.

The effects of domestic protectionism have been shown up in the energy field as well. The main reason why oil prices tended downwards for such a long time is that the United States, on the pretext of conserving its own resources, exploited them more intensively while protecting them by import quotas. The Middle East, and Venezuela as well, suddenly saw their outlets limited, and their oil exerting growing pressure on coal. In fact, the basic situation underwent a complete change from the time when the United States, because of its increased consumption of oil, became a major importer as well as producer; that's when prices began to rise, well before the Yom Kippur War and the embargoes. Naturally, the producing countries' concerted action accelerated the trend. But between the fifteen-year period in which the price in dollars of a barrel of oil remained constant—that is to say, actually decreased in value—and the two years in which the price increased sixfold, it is easy to see the amplifying effect of the policies which gave the world oil market its marginal character.

Similarly, there is a cleavage to be seen where raw materials destined for industry are concerned. The European Community, which doesn't produce more than a small fraction of its needs, exempts practically all industrial raw materials from duties. Britain used to exempt supplies originating in the British Commonwealth, which thus remained Britain's main supplier. In this respect, its entry into the Common Market eliminates some discrimination; for primary producers as a whole, it should enlarge the regular market. The United States, on the contrary, bears the onus of special responsibility in this area. Unlike the community, it protects its primary production fiercely; this went for oil as well as for textile fibers. One of the effects of this is to increase American costs and to diminish the U.S. competitive capacity. In the field of textile fibers, this policy has not even achieved the maintenance of internal production; with prices too high, cotton production was reduced, to the point where even total consumption decreased, to the benefit of synthetic fibers. In all, the United States now uses fewer natural fibers than Japan.

However, quotas or customs protection are not the only culprits in this area. Even though there is no duty on copper, for instance, there is another mechanism at work here which produces the same fluctuations in imports and the instability of prices. It is by and large the same companies which produce at home and abroad for the American market. As soon as demand starts to falter, the inclination is to maintain the production which is closest to the centers of consumption and thereby save on transportation costs. But there is an even greater tendency to maintain domestic employment and to have the effects of market fluctuations act themselves out on the periphery of the market. The expulsion of American firms from Chile may even have more serious consequences, as the U.S. producers will be inclined to maintain only a minimum of their mining activities abroad and to transfer their sources of supply to Africa.

Instability is thus increased manyfold by explicit or implicit protectionist measures; yet the roots of the problem lie even deeper.

INDUSTRIAL RAW MATERIALS

For industrial raw materials, the relationships are still more complicated; there is an interaction between variations in supply and demand. If one assumed, for example, a constant industrial production in the major developed countries, one would, in time, find several factors pulling demand for raw materials in opposite directions.

Technical progress leads to a reduction in the amount of raw materials and energy needed for any given operation. Prestressed concrete or steel alloys, for instance, can provide the same resistance as their much heavier predecessors; the amount of coke required to produce a ton of pig iron grows smaller from year to year; yields of energy are improved by electrification or closed thermal circuits. To this, of course, must be added the substitution of synthetic products for natural materials; but there it is rearrangement rather than overall reduction which occurs; production of synthetics, moreover, requires coal and, even more, oil and natural gas, the chemical uses of which, though still small, represent a growing fraction of total use.

But of course, there is a limit to spontaneous savings and, in fact, there is a continued increase in demand as the lives of consumer durables and heavy machinery tend to grow shorter and shorter. Fashions as well as production processes lead to increasingly frequent changes of car or refrigerator models. Increased competition thus introduces obsolescence into the materials of production even before wear and tear can take their toll. Undoubtedly, some of the domestic and industrial equipment thrown on the scrap heap is recuperated for whatever raw materials it contains, and in this way competes to a certain extent with the extraction of fresh raw materials. But with labor costs going up, the tendency has been to incinerate or abandon rather than to recycle the obsolete; the shorter lifespan of consumer or producer goods has thus led to an unceasing increase in primary demand.

A fear of shortages, together with ecological concerns, might perhaps some day reverse this trend; perhaps there will be serious efforts to make goods last longer and to recuperate waste materials.

One can try to weigh these phenomena against each other: yesterday's technical progress and its negative effects on demand, as opposed to the positive effects of a shorter life for products and tools; tomorrow's systematic search for voluntary saving, as against the limits of spontaneous saving.

The conclusion will no doubt be that at a fixed rate of industrial production there is an annual decline in the consumption of raw materials. In other words, the market can only be maintained through an industrial expansion which makes up for this initial reduction. A constant demand for raw materials is a function, not of the level, but of the rate of growth of industrial production. If, moreover, there is an increase, however slow, in primary production, a second notch in industrial expansion will be required to absorb this supplement.

To this relationship another may be added. Coal provides a typical example in this respect, and it can be extrapolated. Where it has to be mined at great depth, it is very difficult to reduce production without exposing the pits to flooding and subsequent uselessness. On the other hand, production conditions are very rigid and extraction cannot always be accelerated just when demand increases. This may explain the fact that very small variations in demand can result in a sudden shift between overproduction and shortage. A general inference can be drawn from this observation. Either for technical reasons due to mining conditions, or for economic reasons due to the scattered location of mines, primary production reacts much less easily to variations in demand than industrial production; where capacities can be used to varying degrees, employment can be intensified and supplemented by overtime. It is basically this difference in the elasticity of production which is responsible for the fluctuations in primary products being far greater than industrial ones. Production is slow to adjust itself to demand, so prices go up; when production is high demand may have come down again and prices collapse.

Table 4 shows the link between price variations of raw materials, the index of industrial production in the principal countries or groups of countries; and the lack of adjustment of supply to demand.

What is clear from this is that the greatest contribution that could be made to stabilizing the raw materials market would be through a more rapid and more regular rhythm of industrial growth in the major developed countries. But to alternate between inflation and the restrictive policies used to combat it implies for the primary producers even more disastrous consequences.

The analyses carried out up to now shed some light on a debate which could continue for a long time yet. Two different tenets confront each other in this area. There are at all times, and especially just before an

TABLE 4

Industrial Growth Rates and Prices and Production of Nonferrous Metals

Change of Industrial Production (percent) (1970 = 100)

Country/Products	1969	1970 (Change as from 1969)	1971	1972	1973	1974 (Change over 12 months, 1973)	1975 (first quarter) (Change over 12 months, 1974)
Canada	1.9		5	6.65	9.0	5.9	-6.0
U.S.	2.7		0	8.0	9.25	5.7	-10.7
Japan	16.0		3	6.8	18$2	16.0	-17.4
Total, OECD	2.3		2	5.9	10.2	7.1	-9.6
Europe, OECD	5.6		3	4.9	8.3	6.1	-6.3
EEC	6.2		3	3.9	8.4	5.9	-6.4

Price of nonferrous metals (in U.S. cents, at London)

Product	1969	1970 (Change as from 1969)	1971	1972	1973 (Nov. 73)	1974 (March 74)	1975 first quarter (March 75)	Change over 12 months (1974) March 75	May 75
Copper	64.17	-23.9% 49.02	48.56	-0.94% 80.88	66.5% 103.03	27.4% 124.35	21.2% 60.81	-51.1%	-56.4%
Tin	166.80	-4.9 158.60	171.0	7.9 218.60	27.8 253.5	16.0 373.3	47.6 334.50	-10.9	-25.9
Zinc	13.40	4.3 13.98	17.13	22.5 38.50	124.5 73.34	91.5 73.74	3.2 36.42	-50.6	-57.7
Lead	13.78	-16.0 11.46	13.62	19.5 19.48	42.3 22.14	13.7 32.10	45.0 24.62	-23.4	-36.9

World Production and Change (1,000 tons)

Product	1969	1970 (Change as from 1969)	1971	1972	1973	1974
Copper, 1, 2, 14*	5,100	-4.7% 5,340	5,204	-2.6% 5,816	11.8 6,208	6.8 6,265
Tin, 1, 2, 14, 16*	181	2.8 186	187	0.54 190	1.6 185	-2.6 182
Zinc, 1, 2, 14, 16*	4,060	-3.7 3,910	3,735	-4.5 4,084	9.0 4,244	4.0 4,109
Lead, 1, 2, 14, 16*	2,540	1.95 2,590	2,455	-5.5 2,630	7.1 2,694	2.4 2,614

Source: GATT International Trade 1973, Geneva 1974.
Sources: I. O.E.C.D. Industrial Production Quarterly Supplement to the main economic indicators.
II. IMF, International Financial Statistics, monthly bulletin.
III. U.N. Monthly Statistical bulletin, vol. XXVII, no. 5, May 1974.
*1. China excluded.
2. U.S.S.R. excluded.
*14. GDR and DPR of Korea excluded.
16. Czechoslovakia and Rumania excluded.

UNCTAD conference, those who argue for a wider access to outlets, and those who seek an organization of markets. It should go without saying that these two formulas are not mutually exclusive. Stabilization by stockpiling, that is, by the accumulation of financial resources, can go on for a limited time only, unless wider markets absorb the increased production. On the other hand, a policy of freer access to markets will not reduce basic fluctuations, but only the exaggeration of those fluctuations where imported supplies are concerned.

Policies for the stabilization of commodities or other products invariably require lengthy negotiations. Only three agreements (for wheat, coffee, and tin) have so far been set up; others have broken down and have had to be renegotiated. The International Wheat Agreement was basically concerned with price-setting; it was denounced when increased quantities threatened the floor price, though at one point the agreement found itself bolstered by the European Community's willingness to accept a temporary increase in its own stocks to facilitate the flow of American wheat. The agreement on coffee includes limitations on production or exporting. The most complete of the three is the agreement on tin; and it has been renewed. Stabilization in this case is brought about by the creation of buffer stocks financed by the producers themselves.

Stockpiling Costs

The resistance to international stockpiling methods for an ever more extensive number of products is due in part to a misunderstanding. There is a major fear of the financial cost, as if in fact each time that production overtakes demand there were no inevitable stocking charges anyway, paid for either by the producers, the state, or the customers. If stockpiling were based on rules fixed in advance, it would be far less costly and far more efficient than stock building by private operators. When prices go up dealers hold on to their stocks until they are sure that they have reached a ceiling; when prices go down, they do not replenish their stocks unless they estimate that a floor has been reached. In other words a wide margin of fluctuation occurs before stock building or stock reduction finally brings it to an end. A public decision to destock at a price fixed in advance, to begin restocking at a level also fixed in advance, would diminish the average weight of stocks bearing down on each product's cycle; it would also reduce considerably the margin of price variations.

However, there can be no overall solution unless sufficiently large financial means are found and, furthermore, only if they are not used simply for limiting effects, but to attack the causes. In other words, solutions must be found in the monetary sphere. The ideal way would be to come up with a system which would make it possible to finance fluctuations and at the same time go back to the root of the problem, that is, to contribute to a greater stability in the rhythm of industrial production. For, at least where raw materials are concerned, changes in the pace of industrial activity have serious repercussions on those producers who are least able to cope with them.

In the context of international monetary reform, there are several ideas being considered even now in connection with the development of drawing rights. Some countries have suggested that extra rights be accorded to industrialized countries which increase their foreign aid. But this is a suggestion which is not likely to be acted on; it would transfer the burden of generosity to the international community while each country would still claim the credit. Consideration has also been given to financing stocks by a partial allotment of special drawing rights. The IMF, within the framework of its old statutes and within the limits of its normal resources, has already put together some temporary funds for countries which are suffering from decreases in the quantity or price of their exports as a result of fluctuations affecting primary products. The use of drawing rights would have the advantage of reducing the interest burden and also, in practice, of spreading out the repayments. But mechanisms for linking special drawing rights with their attribution to these compensatory tasks have not yet been foreseen in any detail.

The most radical proposal so far for meeting the double objective of raw materials stabilization and greater stability in industrial growth was put forward by Nicholas Kalder, Albert Hart, and Jan Tinbergen, and subsequently revived by Pierre Mendes France.

The basic idea would be to link the creation of an international currency to the increase and decrease of stockpiling. This special currency would be used to pay for stocking groups of products when demand and prices are low, and to put these products back on the market when prices harden; this newly created currency would thus eventually be duly reabsorbed. Primary products would not be stabilized individually, but rather in groups. The advantage of such a system would be the ease with which it would make funds available for stabilizing stockpiles; the rapidity with which money would be created when economic circumstances weaken, and reabsorbed when the pace speeds up. Compared with all other formulas, this one has the distinctive advantage of effectively maintaining both production and revenues. Its authors point out, moreover, that it would provide for a much wider dissemination of effects similar to those attributed by Ricardo to the gold standard. Ricardo had pointed out that when the price of a reserve metal remains stable, it becomes less profitable to produce it if other prices rise, more profitable, on the other hand, when they go down. In this instance the effects would be the same as with the gold standard; the currency would be based on a real backing and would constitute an automatic stabilizer.

The boldness and novelty of this project should not be allowed to detract from it. If it requires central bankers to change their habits, they'll just have to do so. But there is no getting away from the fact that the proposal does harbor two major difficulties which do not seem to have been overcome. First, since the early 1950s commodity trade has not made up more than a decreasingly small fraction of world trade as a whole. This share has grown somewhat under the effect of spectacular price rises, but in volume it is the trading of manufactured goods which increases most. There is no point in saying that this is only a temporary divergence due to the extensive liberalization of manufactured products, but that it will not have a lasting effect. The experience of groups, like the Common Market or the European Free Trade Association, within which trade barriers have been eliminated, shows that the trade of manufactured goods continues to develop long after quotas and customs duties have been removed. It is competition itself which leads to ever finer specialization and diversification of products. Furthermore, a system of monetary creation founded solely on the development of commodity exports would remain well below the needs of world trade. The authors of the project in fact realized this and reasoned, therefore, that a part of currency creation would still have to be based on credits extended to the states, in particular to help them reabsorb assets in reserve currencies; to this extent, the system would thus be backed by loans and would, therefore, partly retain a fiduciary character. In other words one cannot at the same time claim the advantages of a backing in real terms and that of an automatic adaptation to the needs of expansion.

The second objection one should raise seems to be even more radical. Commodities do not all lend themselves equally to a monetary function. Perishable goods, for instance, must be excluded, since they cannot be stocked. It would also be useless to stockpile products which have too little value compared with their volume and which would, therefore, be too expensive to stock. Commodities whose prices are fixed by intergovernmental agreement and which are, therefore, not representative of fluctuations in general, must be excluded as well. For the same reason one would have to exclude those that have their prices determined by international cartel agreements. And finally, one would also have to exclude products which are subject to extreme fluctuations because they constitute only a narrow marginal element of the international market on which they are traded. If all these factors were conscientiously taken into account, one would have to exclude coal and iron ore (too voluminous); wheat, coffee, and tin (governed by international agreements); oil (quite clearly cartelized); and sugar, the price of which triples or quintuples with far too much ease.

Thus, one of two things would happen: if the group of products selected for the stockpiling scheme fulfills the appropriate technical and economic requirements the price variations which affect it will not necessarily reflect those which affect primary products as a whole; that is, the group would not be representative and any monetary creation based on it would cause further distortions, rather than ease matters. On the other hand, if in order to widen the range of products one were to overlook imperfections in each of the markets concerned, the overall price movement of this enlarged sample would be subjected to warping influences of the peculiar market factors of some of its components. As a result the stabilizing effect on products with unorganized markets would likely be all the more negligible.

Simpler Means

In view of these difficulties, could the same basic objectives not be reached by simpler means? One basic fact must be borne in mind right from the start: price changes of commodities, at least of those used for industry, not only determine the position of their producers, they also are very sensitive indicators of industrial production trends in the developed countries themselves. Prices harden when industrial growth accelerates, prices slump as soon as there is a slowdown. Prices should, therefore, provide the major criterion for deciding on a speedup or a slowdown in the creation of international liquidities.

At the present time international monetary reform is trying to find its way. It is quite clear that a return to the gold standard is impossible: gold has for some time now ceased to represent more than an ever smaller fraction of international reserves; industry and private hoarding absorb almost all of current gold production. The first steps have already been taken to bring international practice into line with what has for some time now been the practice within each country—the creation of liquidities not dependent on the vicissitudes of gold mining but regulated by the various mechanisms of monetary policy. The institution of special drawing rights at the IMF has been encumbered with very complicated details and therefore not easily understood by public opinion. But there is a simple underlying principle: the means for international settlements can be created by agreement and creation can be adjusted at will.

On the other hand, there is a striking contrast between the sophistication of the details for operating the mechanism of special drawing rights and the rudimentary character of the thinking about what the conditions and volume of these drawing rights should be, and even more so about how they should be distributed. In the beginning it was agreed that international liquidity would be increased each year by fixed amounts which would be distributed among the members of the IMF in proportion to their quota within the fund.

It has been seen to what extent these formulas have proved unsatisfactory on all sides. It should have been obvious from the outset that in current circumstances the rights were an auxiliary measure; the sums to be created should not, therefore, have been independent of the development of other reserves, gold, dollars, or credits of international institutions. If anything can be defined, it is a general need for liquidity, not any isolated need for this new form of reserve asset; the drawing rights should, therefore, represent the difference between this total and that which would come from other sources. Such a general projection, moreover, should not define more than a trend; it should be possible for adjustment to take place, as may be required by fluctuations in the level of activity, to slow down or to accelerate the creation of international liquidities. What is finally most extravagant about the whole arrangement is that the richer countries, principally the United States, get the lion's share in this largesse, which is, in fact, a purchase voucher for real resources in the markets of other countries.

It is, therefore, urgent that the relationship of special drawing rights to other sources of liquidity be reconsidered, along with how it should be adjusted in different circumstances, and what the allocation criteria should be. A well thought-out system would quite naturally favor growth as rapid as that which was possible for twenty-five years under the dollar standard; at the same time it would avoid the many crises provoked by the latter. It should provide the means for compensating fluctuations of the commodities even as it gets to the bottom of the problem, that is, stabilizing demand within growth.

The solution seems to stare us straight in the face. As a trend, the creation of special drawing rights should be so calculated as to increase total world liquidity by a percentage, defined for each year, and which could be on the order of 4 percent to 5 percent—with due regard for inflationary or deflationary fluctuations. As drawing rights gradually come to represent an ever growing part of total liquidity, the amounts created will come closer to the supplementary total and will no longer have to be defined by their relationship with reserves drawn from other sources. Second, this method should be combined in a binomial formula, with a positive or negative factor which would be based on the overall price changes of primary products. Third, drawing rights would be granted only to developing countries; industrialized countries would have to earn their reserves, not receive them for free; after all, in the past only very exceptional revaluations of gold brought them such windfalls. Fourth, drawing rights would be distributed among developing countries according to whether the value of world exports of commodities affecting them went up or down; if they fell, they would be entitled to a larger share and, on the contrary, a smaller share if world exports of these products went up. In other words, it would not be a matter of compensating each country for a decline in the value of its exports—which could, after all, be caused by above average inflationary trends or total negligence of external markets. Each country would receive compensation according to its share of the total world export market of the products involved; in this way the diligent ones would benefit and the less active ones would be partially penalized.

The general consequences can readily be imagined. The adjusting mechanism for the creation of liquidities is based on overall changes in the primary products market; there is no difference between products which can be stored and those which cannot; and the distortions that can occur on some of the markets are diffused, whereas, they would have a much greater impact if the range of products were reduced. The fact remains that judgement should where necessary be allowed to temper the automatic nature of the criteria. A sudden crisis in the Caribbean which makes sugar prices skyrocket, or renewed turmoil in the Middle East playing havoc with oil prices, should not lead to automatic adjustments. It would be imprudent to accept such price variations without correction. The most important effect to be sought, of course, is to assure continued development and, therefore, to use monetary mechanisms rather than budgetary procedures to this end; for the first contribute to overall expansion while the second involve sacrifices which are more bitterly debated each year. Here, finally, is the key to more stable and rapid worldwide expansion. By allowing primary producers the means of maintaining their demand, a contribution is made to keeping up the rhythm of industrial growth in the developed world, and as a counterpart demand for primary products is stabilized. This is a formula which not only eliminates the exaggeration of fluctuations as they affect imports, it goes to the very root of the problem.

It used to be the fashion in international institutions to denounce the flagrant inequality in the rapid growth of world trade; the growth of exports has always seemed much greater for the industrialized countries than for the developing countries. Even before the upheavals of 1973 helped some of the Third World leap ahead, any more careful analysis of this situation would have revealed that the gap had already been somewhat lessened. The greatest proportion of high export growth was to be found in intra-EEC trade, in the close trade relations between the United States and Canada, and in the tremendous upsurge of Japanese sales. On the other hand, the export growth of the developing continents had long been held back by the poor performance of Latin America; although the latter has started to catch up. Table 5 lists the rate of growth of world exports from 1960 to 1972, and to 1973, for various groups.

What is much closer to the truth, in fact, is that the industrialized countries' imports of manufactured products originate in other industrialized countries—and the part played by the developing world has remained very small everywhere. (See Table 6.)

INDUSTRIAL DEVELOPMENT

Yet, it is essential that the developing countries increase their exports of industrial products. At the beginning of the 1970s, it was estimated that they could not achieve a 6 percent annual rate of growth unless they managed to increase their exports by 8 percent. Since one could only count on a 5 percent annual increase in the sale of primary

TABLE 5

**Coefficients of Increase of Exports in Value Terms
From 1960 to 1972 and 1973**

Exporter	1960-72	1960-73
World	3.22	4.42
Industrialized countries	3.50	4.78
Underdeveloped countries	2.69	3.73
Socialist countries	2.82	3.82
Industrialized countries		
Intra-EEC	6.00	8.13
Intra-North America	3.75	4.76
Japan	7.20	9.33
Others' exports	2.80	3.92
Underdeveloped countries		
Latin America	2.06	2.59
Asia	3.19	4.62
Africa	2.73	3.86

Source: General Agreement on Tariffs and Trade, *International Trade 1973*, Geneva, 1974.

TABLE 6

**Share of Developing Countries in Industrial Imports (1972 and 1973)
and Coefficients of Increase from 1969 to 1972
and from 1970 to 1973**

Exporter	Share of Developing Countries in Industrial Imports (percent)		Coefficient of Increase	
	1972	1973	From 1969 to 1972	From 1970 to 1973
North America	11.7	13.5	1.9	2.29
Japan	18.1	25.7	1.5	2.9
EEC	4.4	5.8(the Nine) 5.1(the Six)	1.26	1.72(the Six)
EFTA	5.0	2.7(U.K. and Denmark excluded) 5.5	1.16	-1.60(U.K. and Denmark included)

Note: the six include Belgium, France, Germany, Italy, Luxembourg, and the Netherlands. The nine include these countries along with United Kingdom, Denmark, and Ireland.

Source: General Agreement on Tariffs and Trade, *International Trade 1973*, Geneva, 1974.

products, the gap could only be filled if their exports of industrial products grew by 15 percent each year.

Has this conclusion been invalidated by the tremendous increase in the prices of certain primary products? What is now more obvious than ever is that one cannot lump together countries which include on the one hand the primary beneficiaries of price increases and those, on the other, which are hardest hit by them, both in terms of industrial price increases as well as raw materials increases. The situation has, therefore, only been aggravated. The newly rich suddenly can afford all the equipment they need, brand-new factories all set up and ready to go, as well as the necessary advice and know-how. Even though in the long run they may fear the exhaustion of their natural resources and, sooner or later, a price slump, for the moment their need for industrial installations is not that great. Nonetheless, they consider that the way to extend their period of growth is to draw the maximum advantage from their present balance-of-payments surpluses. Iran and Algeria, for example, have adopted this policy; even Saudi Arabia, despite its small population, is bent on establishing basic industries, oil refineries, petrochemical plants, and even steel complexes. On the other hand, those countries which are most acutely in need of this type of development, because their traditional deficit makes them all the more dependent on industrial exports, now find themselves less than ever able to acquire the means of industrial production. Whether the newly rich institute new aid programs, or the industrialized countries borrow in order to maintain their own, the fact remains that in this new context development aid takes on even greater importance and urgency.

The fact that a number of countries must have recourse to industrial production in order to grow is a result of the limited employment that agriculture or the extractive industries can offer. In these circumstances, advances in productivity only serve to transform work into a kind of disguised unemployment. It is only industrial production, and the services which it requires, that can absorb unlimited supplies of labor. All the developing countries have tried to take this path to some extent. The means they have, as a rule, chosen are those of import substitution. There is, of course, nothing wrong with this in principle. To begin with any industrial production is a substitute for imports. As soon as there is a local demand, local production replaces imported goods. Such a process cannot of course be initiated without some form of protection. No one questions the fact that industries cannot be born fully grown and need time to reach the scale which makes them economic. Without protection against their more mature competitors, they could never get a start. But much of their development is determined by the extent and duration of their initial protection, as well as by the size of their market. What has happened in almost all countries is that protectionist measures have been established at all levels and have been progressively reinforced, so that in some cases they amount to 300 percent or even 1,000 percent or more. Such industries could, almost by definition, never become exporters. Conversely, an increase in exports is facilitated by a decrease in protection as illustrated by Brazil. Equally disastrous are attempts at autarchy by countries far too small to be able to provide the necessary economies of scale. In such cases, once again, it is inconceivable that domestic production could ever provide the necessary thrust for exports.

Balance-of-payments difficulties have often been used to justify these policies; whereas more detailed analyses have demonstrated that net savings on imports are often much less than the gross figure of domestic production which is supposed to have replaced them, since raw materials or semifinished products or even more so machinery and replacement parts are often themselves imported. Thus it is these very policies and their incoherence which are largely responsible for increasing rather than decreasing dependence on foreign imports; by their very nature they must sustain imports in order not only to cover needs but also to sustain employment, artificial as it may be. How can such policies ever produce an industrial model which will, at the right time, be able to orient itself towards exports? It is clear that for this, any country seeking to industrialize itself will need not only a large enough base but also a certain opening to outside markets.

INDUSTRIAL POLICY

Hollis Chenery and Helen Hughes have done a study for a meeting organized by the World Bank, in which they show that the objective conditions of each developing country in fact explain the outlook and level of its industrialization far better than any defects in its government policies. The objective criteria they developed led Chenery and Hughes to a number of generalizations and classifications. For instance, they concluded that when per capita revenue exceeded $50, small industries started to crop up, to satisfy simple needs such as food, drink, and clothing. At the level of $100, industrial production began to represent some 20 percent of the value of total production, but continued to remain essentially oriented towards the local market. Industrial production did not catch up with primary production until national income reached $400 per capita; and industrial exports didn't reach the level of primary exports before national revenue had attained $900 per inhabitant, per year.

In addition to these averages there are two other criteria which explain the significant differences in market behavior: the size of the countries involved and the availability of important natural resources. Thus the smaller and least well-endowed countries will become industrial exporters rather early; often their industrial sales abroad will reach $10 per capita even before their national income has reached $200. On the other hand, when they have resources, it isn't until they have reached a revenue of $350 that their foreign sales figures achieve a similar level. Furthermore, countries of more than 15 million inhabitants are usually able to reach a point where they can become more quickly competitive on industrial export markets; however, as a rule they will not make the effort as long as their own resources allow them to cover their imports through primary exports.

This explains why the first wave of developing countries which managed to launch themselves on the path of industrial export growth were Hong Kong, Israel, Taiwan, South Korea, and Singapore; and the second wave, much larger countries, like Yugoslavia, Pakistan, Brazil, Colombia, and Mexico.

In some cases the results are quite extraordinary. Israel's exports have had a regular growth of 20 percent per annum. Taiwan and South Korea have broken all records with rates of 35 percent or 40 percent. When Brazil made important changes in its external trade policy, its industrial export figure managed to triple in one year.

Experiences such as these demonstrate quite clearly that it is not the extent of the world market which establishes limits. Figures for 1970 reveal that developing countries account for only 5 percent of world exports in chemicals, 2 percent in iron and steel; whereas their share of nonferrous metals is considerable; of manufactured products other than chemicals and steel they provided only 12 percent of the total, two-thirds of this share being taken up by the developing countries of South and East Asia. Even more striking is the fact that four small Asian countries, South Korea, Taiwan, Hong Kong, and Singapore, export altogether more industrial products than all of Latin America. It is true, of course, that all of them profited from American military activities during the Vietnam war; in addition, Hong Kong and Singapore had preferential access to the British market. However, all things taken together, one must take into account the tremendous effects of the industrial policies within these countries.

Protectionist methods in a number of developing countries have been analyzed very carefully by Bela Balassa. There is no limit, Balassa found, to the costs that one tolerates in certain industries while pretending to develop them, be it through import embargoes, stringent quantitative restrictions, excessive customs duties, arbitrary customs surcharges, obligatory and interest-free advance deposits for imports, and finally, even, exchange rate manipulations. Moreover, the more a country protects the manufacture of components, the more it is forced to increase its protection on the final product in order to compensate its high production cost. It is not rare to find cases where domestic prices of materials and components often exceed that of the final product on the world market. In other words, the true value added is negative. Thus, the policy in certain Latin American countries to insist on a continually increasing proportion of national content in the assembling of cars is likely to have disappointing effects on growth.

Progress is always rapid in the first phase of industrialization, since it deals with relatively simple products But very soon one comes up against the limits of the domestic markets. The transition to the production of intermediate or durable consumer goods, and finally to machinery, requires much more capital and technological sophistication. In other words, in activities where economies of scale are more important, the latter can only be dispensed with at prohibitive costs. Having to invest more to make production more efficient implies that at a certain rate of investment there is a slowdown in the growth of production. At that stage, neither growth nor employment can any longer be assured. At the same time, the distribution of income becomes more unequal. Monopoly profits are guaranteed by protective measures, wage raises are limited because of the ceiling imposed upon productivity, and even agricultural products are then often taxed to finance an autarchic industrial policy. Finally, the workers end up having to pay higher food prices which go to pay for more expensive and shoddier industrial goods.

The effects can be disastrous even on the balance of payments. While the need to maintain a balance has often been used as an alibi for import substitution policies, it is too often forgotten that a number of raw materials, semifinished products, and machinery must be bought outside the country. At any rate, it should be obvious that industries which are developed within a hermetically sealed structure, with artificially inflated operating costs, have little hope of achieving real export potential. If, moreover, such autarchic industries have been developed through foreign investment, the repatriation of profits will only be an added burden to the balance of payments.

Furthermore, the effect will be to divert capital and manpower from those activities where they would enjoy more of a comparative advantage. Thus, indirectly, export potential is even further reduced. This phenomenon is all the more obvious to the extent that measures of industrial protection tend to drive the national currency's rate of exchange much higher than what it would be in a near-free trade situation. Thus, another obstacle in the path of developing competitive export capabilities.

PREFERENCES

Yet, rather than questioning the value of these policies, the under-developed world has found it easier to turn on the industrialized countries and ask them for preferential access to their markets. It is really an accident of history, though, which has oriented developments in this direction and has put the emphasis on the granting of generalized preferences to Third World producers.

In the terms of its association agreements with former colonial territories, the European Community had included the products of these territories, mainly African, in its common external tariff, all the while assuring them of free access. The result was that in every case a preference was established equivalent to the tariff itself. During the preparation of the first UNCTAD, the Latin American countries made it very clear that they fervently wished to see this discrimination disappear; for in their eyes it certainly constituted discrimination against, for example, their coffee, pineapples, or bananas. The Africans, however, were not ready to give up their advantage, which they considered justified because of their lower degree of development, unless it could be compensated by financial assistance which, in the event, went far beyond what Europe was prepared to grant. The compromise arrived at was that Africa could keep its special preferences—which had in the meantime lost some of their value as duties on coffee and cocoa were reduced; the Third World as a whole would ask the industrialized world to scale down or eliminate its tariffs on Third World exports. Thus, the idea of generalized preferences was born—as a reaction and complement to special preferences.

Australia had already taken certain initiatives in this regard. But what would the major importers do—the European Community, the United States, Japan? It wasn't until 1971, seven years after the first UNCTAD, that Europe and Japan developed their first generalized preference schemes. As for the United States, nothing has yet been done, though the Trade Reform Act contains certain special provisions which await ratification. At any rate, it is clear that the United States intends to refuse to apply these provisions to developing countries which, in exchange for special preferences, grant inverse preferences to some industrialized countries. The fact that the African countries at which this is aimed have only very modest trade with the United States indicates that this U.S. position reflects a matter of principle much more than one of real national interest. The worst aspect of this is that the American policy would except just those products which developing countries, thanks to their low-cost labor and simpler technology, are able to produce more advantageously; for example, textiles and shoes. Thus, instead of lowering preferential tariffs on these products, it places them under a constant threat of renewed quota restrictions.

What the European Community, for its part, has done indicates to what extent it is more concerned with political cosmetics than economic effects. The difficulties that had to be overcome and the way advantages had to be distributed among beneficiaries illustrate quite clearly the limits of this method for promoting development.

Even though the generalized preference scheme came about as a result of a compromise between Latin America and Africa, and even though it was debated endlessly at the United Nations, it could not formally be put into effect until a decision had been taken by the GATT; after all, it implied a derogation from the most-favored-nation clause, in that tariffs would be reduced in favor of certain countries without automatically benefiting all the others. During the debate on the question, the associated countries of Africa demanded that the derogation be kept in effect for as short a duration as possible—some spoke of a period of one year. Obviously, any such limitation would have nullified the very aim of the scheme since it would have discouraged any investment tending to build up additional exports. The period that was finally agreed upon was ten years; but the associated countries abstained, as did Greece, Israel, Malta, Portugal, and Turkey, none of which expected to be among the beneficiaries.

The community's scheme was adopted on March 30, 1971, and revised every year. Again, it was a matter of political compromise: only countries which have been recognized by their peers as developing countries can be designated as beneficiaries, that is, the UNCTAD group of 77, which has since become 97. As they would not admit Israel, Israel is excluded but benefits nonetheless, along with North Africa and Spain, from a preferential agreement with the community. On the other hand, even the newly rich oil producers are recognized as developing countries and entitled to preferences.

The whole thing might have been limited to manufactured products. The associated countries would have had nothing to fear in that case, since they supply scarcely 1 percent of the community's imports in this area. The community made a big show of its audacity in including agricultural products and raw materials. In fact, the latter create no problem whatever for it, since the common external tariff is generally zero in this field. Agricultural products, on the other hand, raise an entirely different problem, as the community has the most protectionist policy of all in this area. These tariffs were, therefore, not eliminated but simply reduced and complemented by a safeguard clause; that is, as soon as imports disturb or threaten to disturb community production, preferential rights can be suspended. This is nothing new; safeguard clauses are standard equipment in the GATT repertoire.

What really matters though, is what is done for semifinished or manufactured products. Developing countries benefit from zero tariff rates in this area as well, but only on limited quantities. Duty-free quantities are established on the basis of the latest figures available on community imports from the countries in question; these are increased by an amount equal to 5 percent of the imports from other sources, including the associated states. The community has, since the adoption of its scheme, adjusted this supplementary quantity on the basis of the latest available statistics. In fact, this supplementary amount is regularly increased thanks to the increase in trade among developed countries. It could thus act as a useful multiplier of basic trends, and it was supposed to be applied without exceptions. In practice, however, a special regime has been developed for textiles: tonnage is limited and only basic quantities are used for calculating quotas—no supplementary allowances are made for growth. Special limitations were later applied to plywood as well. This time it was not to protect community industry but the interests of suppliers in the associated countries.

In other words, what the community has instituted is a system of tariff quotas at a customs duty rate of zero. It is a technique which has become customary since the 1957 Treaty of Rome: low or nil tariffs, but on limited quantities of imports—a typical sort of compromise between the principle of a common tariff and the requirements of some member countries to be able to maintain for a while their imports from traditional sources. The method was to be used again when three additional members joined the community. There is a difference, however, in the way it has been applied to the generalized preferences. Tariff quotas usually included a community quota in addition to one for each member state, but as far as the generalized preferences are concerned, this aspect of the formula was to come into practice only in 1975; so far it has not yet been applied. Each member state has its own quota; there is no common reserve and what is not used up in one country cannot be transferred to another.

A number of quotas have, in fact, not been filled. The experience thus justifies a number of criticisms leveled at the formula from the outset. Waiving tariff duties by granting preferential access gives the beneficiary an advantage over other exporters; however, it in no way guarantees that he will be able to compete with the importing country's own producers. Yet without such a guarantee, all the preferences in the world wouldn't be enough to give him a truly effective access to the markets.

This distribution of tariff quotas among member countries has, moreover, entailed another paradox; some of them demanded very large quotas on products which they had been used to importing duty free; this was particularly the case with two of the three newcomers, Britain and Denmark. The latter jumped at the chance of supplying itself with cheap textiles; Britain, to be able to continue its imports from Hong Kong. A distortion was thus introduced into the common external tariff.

As for the effects on the developing countries, the consequences of this kind of ceiling on duty-free imports are considerable. As soon as a quota is filled, subsequent goods are subjected to normal customs duties. The long distances that some of these goods have to travel introduce much uncertainty in this respect. In general, however, the repercussions are even more serious. It has been argued that general preferences require the maintenance of an external tariff, otherwise they would lose their raison d'etre. In fact, the reverse is probably closer to the truth. As long as duty-free quotas remain limited as to quantity, a tariff barrier remains, and constitutes an even more insurmountable obstacle for the less advanced producers.

Yet another experience bears out the predictions made by those who had from the outset questioned the value of a general preference scheme. The community had introduced a check on the system, the purpose of it being that on a general quota offer to the underdeveloped world, no individual country could absorb more than a fraction, which was at first fixed at 50 percent and subsequently reduced for a number of products. As it turned out, practice has borne out what initial analyses foreshadowed. Some countries, like Yugoslavia or Brazil, have been the de facto beneficiaries of a system which claimed to be of general benefit.

Moreover, the system had to be refined by more precise provisions and definitions of products. Otherwise, the developed countries could have ended up benefiting from preferences not intended for them, since all they would have had to do would have been to have their goods transit through the territories of developing countries. Hence, rules of origin were developed to allow for developing-country-content to be identified. To determine the degree to which a product has been upgraded, it was at first considered sufficient for it to have moved from one customs category to another. Unfortunately the community's tariff did not provide, within all its branches, categories for each level of upgraded product. It thus adopted as a criterion the percentage of value added. Suddenly countries like Singapore, which had no raw materials, found themselves threatened with exclusion. The idea thus evolved to the point where one took into account the overall value added when a product went through several stages of processing in different countries belonging to the same regional union. And the stage has now been reached where it is envisaged that there should be a totting up of "values added" which the same product accumulates through successive stages in several developing countries. All this is very logical but impossibly complex when it comes to applying it.

A Misdirected Effort?

However well intentioned the promoters of generalized preferences may have been, one asks oneself if the whole thing wasn't launched in the wrong way. Its limitations, after all, were foreseeable. There are countries and products which cannot compete with the local producers of import markets. No preference over other exporters can, therefore, guarantee them access to markets. As the experience of a number of unfilled community quotas has demonstrated, the advantages from a preference can remain nothing but a pure formality. What is worse is that the gaps between the developing countries themselves are thus widened. It is the more advanced countries which can take advantage of additional markets, whereas the others are discarded by excessive costs of incipient industries. Thus, the advantages that the first group has over the second tend to grow cumulatively—as they manage to increase their exports thanks to preferences they also manage to develop economies of scale and reduce production costs. The new chasm that is thus being opened may result in the countries already least favored finding themselves suffering from an even more retarded development.

Yet, the Third World constitutes less than ever a homogeneous bloc. The gaps between its various countries, even more so between its various regions, are perhaps even wider than the gap which exists between what are generally called the developing world and the industrialized world. Moreover, with the general preference scheme, one comes up against the never ending difficulty of having to agree on criteria by which one or another country would be prevented from claiming the privileges that go with the status of underdevelopment. The real problem should be how to make the access to markets itself pass progressively from one group of countries to another, less favored group, and so on.

In the final analysis, no country can make reasonable investment plans on the basis of preferences subject to quantitative ceilings. After all, what options does a country have if in the time it takes to transport its goods to a preferential market, quotas have been filled by deliveries from other countries? It is obvious, therefore, that the system of generalized preferences—which the United States has not yet seen fit to apply—is already in need of being replaced, or at least improved by the application of new formulas. Its objective should be threefold: first, to allow for an effective access to the markets of advanced countries for the new industries of developing countries; second, to lend itself to an automatic reduction of such facilities as a developing country progresses along its industrial path—in this way other countries would not be deprived of this much needed access; and third, to allow for a rational division of labor not only for limited quantities of products but for entire industries.

An Atlantic Institute study on a monetary policy for Latin America has provided an outline of an answer to the first two problems. The study recognizes a fundamental paradox and bases its answer thereon. In general it is admitted that newborn industries have a right to at least temporary protection. But the consequences of this are not usually drawn. The products of such industries have no chance of penetrating external markets unless they are subsidized. However, international rules, in principle at least, prohibit export subsidies. In practice, they are tolerated in the case of developing countries. What results is anarchy. The majority of countries do not grant themselves the means for gaining access to external markets; whereas some of them take unlimited advantage of them. International competition is thus thoroughly perverted.

A DUAL SYSTEM

It was, therefore, proposed that a fundamental dualism be recognized in the case of the developing countries. There is a kind of conflict within most of their economies between, on the one hand, a traditional sector of exports, made up essentially of primary products and sometimes of fairly primitive industrial goods and, on the other, incipient industries. If the international community could be brought to recognize this reality, some order might be established. It would then be obvious that these new sectors and the traditional ones should not be treated in the same way. At the same time, care would be taken not to allow a multiplicity of arbitrary practices to crop up in order to compensate for particular difficulties or inefficiency.

In other words, recognition of this fundamental dualism between a traditional sector and new ones would lead to dual exchange rates or similar measures, but would rule out the use of multiple exchange rates.

In fact, when a country is in the early stages of industrialization and trying to protect its early growth, a currency devaluation aimed at restoring its balance of payments can quickly turn against it. Strictly speaking a devaluation will be effective in opening new markets only under certain conditions. First, as in the case of fairly advanced countries, they must already have a considerably varied range of products to sell abroad. This is, of course, the case for developed countries and is also true for Mexico which, thanks to the Latin American free trade area, has been able to increase its industrial exports substantially. Brazil is gradually coming into this category after having made tremendous strides in developing its sales of manufactured products. Second, a single, devaluated exchange rate can be maintained to facilitate exports in circumstances where primary products exports constitute the bulk of foreign sales and can be further developed without competing with other products, for instance by putting heretofore uncultivated land into production; unless this condition is met any expansion of primary production in general can only occur at the cost of reduced food production for local consumption; the higher costs of imports due to the devaluation would then only be aggravated by domestic shortages. The third condition must be that the country concerned does not have a decisive influence on the international market; otherwise, its devaluation would bring about a lowering of the world price of its product, for example, Brazil in the case of coffee or Ghana in the case of cocoa. The final condition is that the country not be too dependent on imports which have a direct effect on the cost of living, that is, food products; otherwise the benefits of a devaluation would quickly be lost through wage increases.

Clearly these conditions are rarely ever all present in any developing country. Once again, one comes up against a fundamental predicament; that which needs to be protected against imports cannot be exported unless it is somehow subsidized so as to make up for domestic costs which exceed those of the world market.

To get around this problem, there are several useful techniques which can be applied. The choice of one or the other will depend on the administrative makeup of the country concerned and also on the variety and importance of the products to be exported.

The simplest and most elegant formula is that of a dual exchange rate. On one side traditional exports would be quoted at the higher foreign currency rate, that is, they would bring in that much less local money for an equivalent amount of foreign earnings. On the other hand, new exports would be quoted at a preferential rate and would thus earn more local currency for an equivalent amount of foreign exchange. To avoid, as much as possible, the inflationary effects of exchange rates, the purchase of essential imports should benefit from the favorable rate of exchange so that they will cost the very least in terms of local currency; whereas the rate applied to new exports, that is, more foreign exchange against local currency, would also be applied to nonessential imports. It is easy to see that it thus becomes possible to adjust the difference between the two rates by varying the lists of products to be privileged for export and those of imports which are to be privileged or penalized. As new exports grow, be they primary products not traditionally sold abroad, or manufactured products, the exchange rate of the local currency will tend to climb. Thus the tendency will be to return to a single exchange rate and this will have come about thanks to development caused by the dual exchange rate itself.

This sort of technique should only be used, however, in countries which have sufficiently refined mechanisms for manipulating exchange rates and which seek to export a relatively large number of products. The typical situation in most underdeveloped countries is that they draw their foreign income from a single primary product and that they have few other products, either primary or manufactured, which they could hope to develop for export. In such cases it is simpler to adopt a single exchange rate, fixed somewhere between that which would make the traditional product competitive and that needed for other products. Taxes could be levied on traditional exports in order to subsidize new ones. One rule must be adhered to however: the export subsidy must not be greater than the amount of effective protection given the product on the domestic market. Another rule is that the subsidy must be covered by the taxes derived from traditional exports. In such conditions export subsidies aim only at correcting the relative disadvantage to which new industries are exposed; they are, therefore, in no way arbitrary. As economies of scale begin to develop, the necessary degree of protection decreases; as external sales grow, subsidies per unit grow smaller since new exports begin to catch up with those of the traditional products which help to pay for them. Once again the mechanism would wither away as a result of its own success.

Rules of this kind would bring some order into a world where some make no move to help their own exports while others subsidize them to excess, and yet others get caught up in the chaos of multiple exchange rates. Unlike the preferential scheme, they would also prevent further splits between developing countries. The growth of exports in countries eligible for a dual exchange rate would of itself gradually eliminate the latter and bring about the promotion of their countries' economies to a more advanced state, with more diversified exports and a single exchange rate. At the same time thanks to these efficient mechanisms, one after another among new, less advanced countries would gain access to industrial markets.

Measures of Protection

All this assumes, of course, that the industrialized countries do not block access to their markets by continuing to overprotect their weakest industries. They have, after all, not abandoned the practice of quantitative restrictions, which continue overtly in the form of import quotas or under the more hypocritical guise of voluntary restrictions applied by the exporting countries themselves (see Table 7).

As for tariff barriers, nothing is more difficult than to estimate their average level. If one goes about it by calculating an arithmetic average of

TABLE 7

Main Quantitative Import Restrictions

Product	Germany	France	Italy	Belgium	U.S.	U.K.
Primary products[a]						
Non agricultural materials						
Coal	X	X		X		X
Oil		X			X	
Agricultural raw materials						
Cotton, long fibers					X	
Cellophane		X				
Cork			X			
Manufactured products[b]						
Textiles	X	X	X			
Manufactured jute	X	X		X		X
Radio components		X				
Aircraft and spare parts		X				X
Chemicals; butter substitutes					X	

[a] Coming from Japan, underdeveloped countries.
[b] Coming from Japan, Hong Kong.
Source: Compiled by the author.

all duties levied in every customs area, one ends up attributing the same value to major categories as well as to negligible items. If one tries to come up with a weighted average by using each customs area's particular imports, one obtains extremely disparate and underestimated results, since import volumes are generally much greater when there are low or no duties in effect, and, at the same time, very little weight is given to extremely high duties. A somewhat more balanced solution would use a weighting formula based not on each area's particular imports, but on the part that each product represents in international trade. However, in so far as protectionist systems in the more important markets all resemble each other, any weighting would produce the same distortion in each customs area. In the final analysis, a true measure of protection would have to take into account, under every tariff category, the corresponding consumption within the importing country; only in this way could one get an idea of the extent of any potential market. The GATT has tried the first three sorts of calculations noted here but the last one, the most significant, has never yet been attempted.

Entirely different results are obtained depending on whether one applies total customs revenue to all imports or to dutiable items only. The second figure would, of course, be considerably higher than the first. Depending on what weighting method is used, average duty rates also turn out to be very varied.*

It must also not be forgotten that the average of a tariff does not really reflect the protection it affords. The more diverse a tariff, the higher its protection, particularly if it contains sharp peaks compared to the average rate. Here are a few random examples: the community's duties on mineral and fertilizer products can go up to 30 percent, as compared to an average rate of 5 percent; on the same items, American rates climb up to 100 percent; on transport equipment, community rates are on average 8 percent with peaks at 30 percent; on shoes and travel goods the U.S. rate is, on average, 12 percent but climbs to 50 percent at certain points, as well as on various other manufactured items.†

What is most striking is that the most excessive duty rates are levied on textiles, leather goods, clothing, that is, all those items which can most easily be supplied by developing countries. The outlook is even darker when one realizes that these same items are handicapped even further by quantitative restrictions, exceptions to the general preference scheme or by voluntary export restrictions. Furthermore, one must not forget that a characteristic aspect of textiles made from natural fibers is that the imported raw material constitutes a substantial part of the

---

*See Pierre Uri, *Rapport sur la capacite concurrentielle des Communautes europeennes:* table, page IV.2.51 showing the lowest and highest averages obtained by different methods of calculation and applied, on the one hand, to total imports and, on the other, to dutiable imports only. Comparisons are made between EEC tariffs and those of Great Britain before it joined the Common Market, and of the United States and Japan.

†See Pierre Uri, *Rapport sur la capacite concurrentielle des Communautes europeennes* page IV.2.52. This tables gives a simplified measurement of this tariff dispersion by showing in each category the highest rates. In each case two characteristic figures are given which are applicable to substantial volumes of imports.

product's value. When raw materials are imported duty free, a 15 percent protection on the price of the final product represents 30 percent of the value added, if the value added is only one-half of the whole product. If, in addition, one applies quantitative restrictions, outside competition is even further frustrated and the split between internal and external prices is widened even further.

All these considerations are systematically taken into account in the present definition of effective protection. This effective protection can be lower than the nominal rate of duty when costs are increased by duties in effect on the raw materials, semifinished products, or equipment used in the production of the item in question. By adding up all these factors weighted by their incidence on costs, one can figure out the remaining protection in regard to value added. To some extent protective measures, when applied too generally, may partially cancel themselves out.

Another consequence of this definition is that it integrates customs duties and quantitative restrictions, the effects of which it finds reflected in price differences. One way of having a general yardstick for effective protection might be by measuring the excess of value added in domestic prices over what it would be in international prices. This difference would reflect the effect of quantitative restrictions as much as that of customs duties, even after duties on component parts have been deducted. However, complications do not stop here. Two further corrections must be made. Where monopolies are involved, domestic prices may be raised beyond what protective measures alone would have made possible. The two effects must be considered separately. Furthermore, the lowering of protection can require balance-of-payments adjustments in the form of devaluation; consistency would then require that one reduce the nominal value added surplus in relation to the potential change in parities.

The advantages and difficulties of this type of more rigorous measurement of the effects of commercial policy are immediately apparent. It has a twofold practical implication. The smaller the value added factor of one sector, the higher the relation to it of the customs duties levied on the price of the product. The overall industrial figures available are not sufficiently subdivided to bear out this fact clearly in every case. One can cite, for example, Japanese data where the flour milling industry shows valued added figures of only 6 percent; in U.S. or European Community data, oil products are listed as having a value added of only 11 percent or 21 percent, respectively. In the field of metal smelting, it is unfortunate that the production of pig iron or copper refining are not shown separately from the overall production of steel or nonferrous metals. It would allow for fuller conclusions to be drawn on the effects of duties on such initial upgrading when the raw material content is entirely duty free. The community has imposed some limits on the tariff levels that may be applied to semifinished products. But even a duty of only 5 percent amounts to 100 percent protection on value added, if the initial upgrading adds only 5 percent to the value of the product.

OPENING THE MARKETS

The underdeveloped countries are accused of doing too much import substitution where finished products are concerned. What one should ask oneself, however, is whether other options are open to them. Are there sufficient outlets to make it possible for them to plan on industrializing their economies on the basis of natural resources and the first stages of processing? There is nothing rational about having to import coal, ore, and labor rather than importing pig iron which would cost less to transport. Furthermore much of the initial processing of raw materials requires large-scale energy consumption. At the same time, the developed countries are worried by the dramatic environmental implications of an exponential growth in energy needs, whether they are satisfied by oil or by nuclear power.

In many respects the situation is something of a scandal. The industrialized countries have succeeded in forming regional groups and even in agreeing on reduced customs duties between trading blocs; they have thus recognized the importance of an international division of labor, as well as the usefulness of competition in encouraging advances in productivity; they have also learned that specialization can result in the consumer's having access to a wider variety of products. Yet, as soon as this sort of distribution of activities could benefit the poorer countries, it is refused to them. In fact, it is here that it would be most beneficial. The greater the difference in the conditions of production, the more sense there is to trade—provided, of course, that the process of adaptation be sufficiently gradual, since any traumatic transformation would only produce reaction and retard liberalization for much longer.

Does the plan exist which would make it possible to have a truly rational division of labor, to the advantage of all those involved? Tinbergen has tried to formulate some basic principles in this respect. He bases himself on the theory of comparative advantages and how it can be interpreted in terms of the relative abundance of production factors. He goes on to calculate for different industries the relationship between capital requirements and labor requirements and, for a whole series of countries, the relative abundance of shortage of one or other of these factors. This approach is, of course, more valuable as a quantified experiment and as a methodological effort than in terms of immediately applicable results. The data on the costs prevalent in various industries and on the capital resources of each country is terribly hazardous. Perhaps the new realities of the world in which we live will allow for a more simplified version of this rather complicated calculation.

With today's almost frightening capital mobility, one cannot consider capital as a fixed factor in a country's resources. The same goes for management know-how and technology, which can be transferred with each through multinational enterprises. Hence, more and more it is work itself which becomes the decisive factor.

In a study on the imports of manufactured products from developing countries, H.B. Lary tries to bring some rational interpretations to the question; he categorizes industries according to the proportion of labor in their value added. His conclusion was that the most developed countries, where advances in productivity made labor continuously more expensive, would gradually have to abandon those branches of activity where labor accounted for the highest part of value added, and to direct themselves towards those where capital plays a more decisive role. To take this argument to its ultimate conclusion, the industrialized world would either find itself confronting an insoluble employment problem or else resolutely adopting a policy of reducing working hours and developing leisure.

However, if one examines realities more closely, one may discover an entirely different way out. Labor is not a homogeneous factor. Within a single national economy all jobs are not equally remunerative. In the United States, in Western Europe, as much as in Japan, one is struck by the extraordinary disparity between wage scales in different branches, in different regions, and even between different companies in the same branch.

Roughly speaking wages within a branch are directly related to the size of enterprises. The highest wages paid in the smallest and largest firms can vary by as much at 20 percent; even 45 percent in Japan. Between branches the disparity is, of course, much greater. Even if one excludes the extreme examples of electricity or the oil industry, where labor costs are of only marginal importance, wages vary from one to two-and-a-half times. The scale is, of course, much tighter in a highly integrated economy such as that of Germany; it is much more widespread where great differences separate modern sectors and enterprises from generally unadapted industries. Disparities between branches can result from a number of basic differences: regional variations, the quality of labor required, in many cases the proportion of female labor employed, the average size of enterprises which in turn differs among sectors.

The European Community has done an in-depth study which has revealed that in relation to an average wage index of 100 (social security and other employer contributions included) the disparities for workers in

different industries included the following: 75 for footwear and clothing in
Germany, 65 in France, 73 in Italy, 61 in the Netherlands, and 65 in
Belgium; the figures for coal mining were 126, 151, 156, 148, and 129 in
the same countries; for oil they were 123, 170, 157, 193, and 167. In the
United States leather and textiles measure up to only 72 compared to the
average, the automotive industry 127, and steel, as well as oil refining,
132. Wages in service industries like hotels or dry-cleaning establishments
were by comparison, even lower. When it comes to Japan, the disparity
goes from 55 for the clothing industry to 150 for electricity; within these
two extremes lie 127 for the steel industry and 122 for oil, even though all
this only accounts for companies employing at least 30 people. The disparity between wages in Japan is thus very underestimated in the data,
since it is generally known that wage differences between the smallest
concerns and the others are very big indeed.*

Labor's Interests

It is amazing that it should have taken so long before anyone drew
conclusions from such startling facts. It should go without saying that it
is in the interests of labor progressively to withdraw from activities
which are no longer able to pay more than the most inadequate wages.
This does not imply, however, that on the whole there will not be enough
employment. The line should be drawn between those jobs which require
the most menial type of labor and those which require increasingly higher
qualifications.

This should not lead to the conclusion that the underdeveloped
countries are perpetually condemned to the more rudimentary forms of
work, while the developed countries can offer their workers the more
advanced and better paying occupations. As it is, a number of Third
World countries have got to the stage where they can produce articles of
the highest technology. But one must think in terms of general trends.

This is the true criterion of an international division of labor. Even
with wages which bear no relationship to those in industrialized countries,
the developing countries can often not compensate for disparities in
productivity which are related to differences in scales of production and
even more to the absence of a sufficiently trained labor force. On the

*See Pierre Uri, *Rapport sur la capacite concurrentielle des Com-
munautes Europeennes:* tables on pp. III.1.63, III.1.65, III.1.67.

contrary, the industrialized countries have managed to maintain their advantage in this field despite unendingly rising wages. No division of activities could, of course, be instituted from one day to the next; what is essential is that it be launched and allowed to progress gradually. However, the conditions for this must be recognized and the consequences fully understood.

The fundamental requirement is full employment. It is only when workers can be secure in this respect that they can be persuaded to abandon their less remunerative jobs and to look upon change as an opportunity for promotion. At the same time, such mutations must be helped along at every stage. The Swedish unions seem to be the ones which have best understood under what conditions labor can be guaranteed the highest level of living. While insisting on the most absolute guarantees for a permanent income and demanding continual professional training and retraining programs, they give their fullest support to gradual transfers of workers from less productive enterprises or centers to the more productive ones. The European Coal and Steel Community introduced a major innovation in this area. The treaty which created it provided for extensive measures in favor of the readaptation of workers who might be displaced by competition or technological progress. It instituted special allowances for workers caught between jobs, but even more important, it provided for special programs to help workers reestablish themselves in a new location or acquire new professional skills where changes of occupation were involved. Similar ideas have been put forward in the context of the Common Market and the creation of the Social Fund. In the Trade Expansion Act, the United States has copied some of these ideas and referred to an "adjustment" process, rather than protectionism. The conditions and procedures for putting these measures into effect were, however, so restrictive that no assistance under this category was ever granted. This deficiency is largely responsible for American unions having returned to their old protectionist evangelism. Fortunately the Trade Act has more flexible provisions on this score.

On a worldwide economic scale no more valuable expenditures could be made, for they insure that structural changes will be accepted; without such changes in structures, growth and advances in living conditions will continue to be blocked.

Nothing can be more important than to convince labor that it must give up its attachment to particular jobs in particular places; such immobility is no longer compatible with inflation-free progress. It is in the interests of the industrialized world as much as of the Third World, to encourage a gradual shift to more highly qualified specialization, to more productive enterprises, to more competitive branches. The effect will be not only to encourage embryonic industries in the developing countries, but also a genuine international division of labor which will make it possible for wage scales everywhere to be adjusted to higher standards. After all, this is one of the conditions of bringing about rapid improvements in the level and quality of life.

The record of the developing world in the field of regional integration is one of more failures, more preliminary unions which came unstuck, more mergers which were doomed as they were signed, than of any real accomplishments. There are or have been no fewer than twenty-seven different regional arrangements; even worse, there is a whole cemetery of defunct or aborted groupings of one kind or another.

French Western Africa created a customs and monetary union which provided for free circulation of goods, uniform external customs duties, and a central issuing authority. No sooner did the former colonies achieve independence than they dissolved the union. Some of them continued to belong to a central bank so that they could benefit from French monetary assistance; others, like Mali, decided to print their own money, but returned to the franc zone soon after. The Mali Federation, between Senegal and the former French Sudan, also turned out to be only an ephemeral event; when it came, the break was so severe that for a long time the Dakar-Bamako railway was closed to traffic. There was at one time an East African economic community among Kenya, Tanzania, and Uganda; it even had some common ministries; but tensions among those countries were such that not much remains of it. On the Asian continent there is an agreement binding Turkey, Iran, and Pakistan to a scheme for creating certain industries; a fairly loose association of the southeastern countries, Thailand, Malaysia, Singapore, Indonesia, and the Philippines, which includes some plans for industrial development, but which has taken years before even giving itself a common secretariat. The federation between Singapore and Malaysia, as we know, fell apart very quickly.

In the Arab world, unions, dissolutions, and regroupings are almost innumerable; Egypt and Syria, Egypt and Lybia, Lybia and Tunisia, without counting the various stillborn attempts to unify the Maghreb.

143

It is only in the relatively more developed continent that it has been possible to carry such schemes a little further. The common market of Central America, however, groups only very small countries and has been shaken by the war between El Salvador and Honduras. There is a more ambitious project for a free trade area for all of Latin America; the beginnings of it, as well as its limits and its perpetually retarded timetable, will be examined in greater detail below. Within this grouping a more resolute effort has, nonetheless, been made to form a subregional union of the Andean group; it goes down the Pacific from Colombia to Chile and has ended up including Venezuela as well.*

It is not self-evident that all these setbacks were necessarily disasters. To group a number of small countries together in an overprotective arrangement may imply that the more advanced ones will run the risk of having their own growth interrupted, whereas it would have been better off linked to the larger and more modern markets of the developed countries. This has been one of the main concerns raised by the creation of a Central American common market and it was precisely for this sort of reason that Singapore broke its ties with Malaysia. Singapore's rate of growth and industrial exports thereafter became one of the highest in the world.

There can be even greater difficulties in this area. If a country decides that it will try to control the rise of inequalities which tends to accompany growth, it can do so only in cooperation with its neighbors. If one of its neighbors, on the other hand, decides to pursue growth at all costs, without any attempt at reducing income disparities, the former will lose its more qualified personnel to the latter. Thus, the more egalitarian countries are threatened with the loss of their most precious human resources unless they close their borders. This is what China has done; it is not, however, a solution easily put into practice in a region like Africa. In the final analysis, a regional community cannot work unless there is a fundamental agreement on the direction and type of development to be pursued.

LIMITS TO REGIONAL TRADE

In fact, wherever one looks one sees that within any developing continent, regional trade accounts for only a small fraction of total exports, as shown in Table 8.

---

*On the different regional groupings in Latin America see Adalbert Krieger-Vasena and Javier Pazos, *Latin America: a Broader World Role* (London: Benn, 1973).

TABLE 8

Ratio of Intraregional Trade to Overall Trade (1972 and 1973) and Coefficients of Increase of Intraregional Trade from 1960 to 1972 and 1973

Region	Ratio of Intraregional Trade to Overall Trade (percent)		Coefficient of Increase of Intraregional Trade	
	1972	1973	From 1960 to 1972	From 1960 to 1973
European Economic Community	49.7	48.8	6.00	8.1
European Free Trade Association	28.6	29.4	3.88	5.2
North America	37.8	33.4	3.75	4.7
Latin America	18.5	16.7	2.24	2.6
Africa	6.0	6.2	2.35	3.0
Asia (Japan excluded)	19.3	17.3	2.43	3.5
Underdeveloped countries	19.2	19.1	2.47	3.1
Socialist countries	61.4	57.0	2.41	3.0

Source: General Agreement on Tariffs and Trade, *International Trade 1973,* Geneva, 1974.

Ten years after the countries of Latin America had signed their free trade Montevideo treaty in 1961—to which Venezuela and Bolivia acceded only later while Central America formed a separate group—the trade between all the member countries amounted to no more than one-fifth of their total foreign trade—it had been one-tenth at the beginning.

The data has to be examined more closely. Relative values change depending on whether one includes or excludes Venezuela. Thanks to its oil resources, Venezuela, by itself, accounts for one-third of all Latin American exports. There is, however, no growth in its trade with the subcontinent. At the same time, the Central American signatories in 1960 of the Treaty of Managua establishing a common market have managed to increase their trade from 5 percent to 25 percent of their total exports. The six original members of the European Common Market each direct on average one-half of their total exports to each other. Enlargement has brought this proportion to two-thirds except for Britain. At the same time as international trade tripled in value, that between the six was multiplied by six.

Some of these comparisons are even more startling. Within Latin America the growth of mutual trade in manufactured products has been slower than similar sales to the rest of the world. This provides some idea of the limits to regional integration in the developing world. To understand these limits better, however, one must bear in mind what each country's objectives are, what obstacles may be foreseen, and the additional difficulties which have come to plague such schemes subsequently.

The idea of tying the Latin American economies closer together is a very old one. The same people who at the Economic Commission for Latin America (ECLA) were urging industrialization have been very quick to recognize the limits to import substitution. They were aware of the historical and cultural factors which favored closer links; more than 200 million people divided into only two main languages, and related ones at that! Yet they were aware of the pitfalls. It goes without saying that any industry in its initial stages in effect produces substitutes for imports. The whole question is whether it limits itself to monopolizing the local market, however narrow it may be. To do so, of course, means disregarding the crucial importance of economies of scale in most industries and the usefulness of competition in promoting more efficient and low cost production methods.

The biggest leap forward in this respect was provoked when the coal and steel community and the more ambitious Rome Treaty gave rise to the powerful European grouping. One of the experts who had helped to bring the successive communities into being was subsequently called upon by Prebisch for his advice. His report and its conclusions were endorsed by a high-level group of experts of the ECLA. His recommendations were in fact not much more than a minimum which was deemed acceptable to the ECLA countries, yet the Treaty of Montevideo did not go even this far. And, as experience has shown many times over, there is a threshold of effectiveness, below which action is doomed to failure.

Let there be no misunderstanding; the project was in no way too ambitious. No one imagined that one could copy in Latin America something which had been possible in much more sophisticated economies with infinitely more diversified exports. Neither the differences nor the obstacles were underestimated. But if European countries with big populations and already well-developed levels of income felt themselves inadequate to compete with the United States, what conclusions, a fortiori, had to be drawn for even the most populated Latin American countries? Brazil, though it boasts 100 million inhabitants, has a GNP not much greater than that of Belgium. At the other end of the scale, how can one build up industries in countries with fewer than 2 or 3 million inhabitants?—where the majority subsist without even having penetrated into a money economy?

No one was fooled into thinking that integration was all that was needed to launch a brand-new kind of industrial progress. Latin America has for a long time traded in foreign markets where it sold its raw materials and from where it imported its manufactured products. Its entire infrastructure was geared towards the outside while internally its communication links remained surprisingly underdeveloped. Even its banking system was primarily linked with the large financial centers abroad. It also goes without saying that vast projects such as the development of large river basins require a certain amount of cooperation and joint planning. The planning and building of this type of infrastructure, as well as its direction, in turn require a certain degree of regional integration. For, in the end, schemes for expanding communications links and investment projects associating a number of countries will all be stillborn if artificial obstacles to foreign trade are not removed.

After all, even Europe has discovered that its Common Market will not continue to thrive unless policies are adopted to bring about a balance between regions and to avoid price disparities which the growth in trade has not managed to eliminate altogether. The difficulties of putting these policies into effect are quite evident and none of it would ever have been envisaged if a link between markets had not been present.

The creation of a regional market in no way implies renouncing the development of trade relations with the outside. There is no contradiction at all between the idea of a common market and increased freedom in overall foreign trade; on the contrary, there should at first be a fairly large base upon which to develop industries able to compete on foreign markets. Thus, it is only for a limited period of time that a regional market can be a form of import substitution, even if this is managed on a collective rather than a narrowly national basis. Regional organization can have the effect of eliminating some effective discrimination even while it introduces an apparent one. Normally, countries try to protect their economies with extremely high barriers which are opposed to competitors, the least redoubtable as well as the best equipped ones. Then only the most industrially advanced countries have any hope of surmounting these barriers. Thus, among countries which have agreed to speed up their industrialization, it makes more sense to grant protection to newborn industries on a collective and reciprocal basis rather than country by country.

THE MARKET SIZE

It must be remembered that the size of a market begins very soon to be a decisive factor. According to a rough rule of thumb, cost prices decline by 20 percent every time production doubles. This is, of course, only an average figure. There are industries where economies of scale are relatively unimportant; for example, the textile, clothing, or leather goods industries. These are the ones that were the first to be developed in narrow markets. But as soon as one leaves this rather limited field, one enters an area where nothing can be produced except within very sizeable units. A study conducted by a group of Latin American research institutes, and coordinated by the Brookings Institution, has given careful consideration to what sort of production could be established on a common basis in the whole of Latin America. Several chemical products, some type of machinery, and pulp and paper were some of the topics which they studied. However, the ratio between cost and plant size varies greatly in these industries. In some cases size may even cause cost increases. For example, for a paper factory to expand, it requires access to large forest reserves which in turn increases its materials transport costs. But in general the study brings out the fact that as plant dimensions increase, regardless of where they are situated, the total cost per manufactured unit can be cut in half or even quartered. It is general knowledge, furthermore, that a steel-making plant which a few years ago could be economically viable with a production capacity of 500,000 tons, now requires more than 1 million; in fact, one tends to think in terms of 3 million tons when setting up any new plant. It is obvious, therefore, that any country wishing to develop along these lines, with a demand that doesn't even approximate the required minimum, raises immeasurable obstacles for itself. The manufacture of automobiles, for instance, requires a flow of about 200,000 units per annum. Similarly, in the field of electrical household appliances technological progress drives the optimal figure higher every year. For there is one general law governing organizations: when the principal manufacturing process makes a step forward, all other related activities must follow. Thus the optimum size for a production unit in any industry is constantly changing—and growing.

These laws are particularly relevant for production goods. This applies to machinery and to intermediate goods, like the processing of metals or chemicals which are derived from each other. They are also valid for parts and components which are combined in any assembly. Did these conclusions justify Latin America's adopting a plan for newborn industries only? In fact, substitution production had everywhere been exaggerated to such an extent that there were only very few industries which were not already in existence, at least in an embryonic state. In any case, such equipment industries could only be envisaged in the larger countries; the process would thus have left most of the Latin American republics behind, most particularly the small or medium-sized ones which are most in need of a wider market to develop their industries.

Moreover, how could one then have developed effective competition?—still the most powerful way to contain cost prices and to improve quality. It was also obvious that the idea of confining common progress to new industries accredited too many hazy fears. An industry can, of course, displace another, but only where demand remains stagnant. However, Latin American demand is potentially quite large. Given sufficiently rapid growth, experience has shown that the addition of new capacities does not make the old ones useless, that existing industries do not disappear, but rather that they become progressively specialized. There is more of an intrasectorial than of an intersectorial division of labor.

There was another reason which argued in favor of a determined effort in this area. Any country which is still dependent on a limited overall production, regardless of how large its territory or population, naturally has only a weak bargaining power. To demand is one thing, but a trade negotiation is an entirely different matter. At every UNCTAD conference, Latin America has distinguished itself in the former field. The European Community, on the other hand, has shown how much power can be derived from a common tariff. It was thus able to set itself and pursue an important primary objective: to get its more important trading partners, particularly the United States, to reduce their protective barriers. Latin America, in spite of all the advice it has been given, has not been able to arm itself with such an instrument.

THE LATIN AMERICAN EXPERIENCE

Latin America's bearing in these matters has been very diffident and the results just as slim, no doubt because each country fears its neighbors even more than the big international competitors. The behavior of local entrepreneurs, labor unions, or even the subsidiaries of foreign companies, notably the U.S.-based ones, have not been very different in this regard. Each industry had established itself behind high protective walls. Vested interests were such, therefore, as to argue against any attempt at integration. Right from the start the reduction of tariff barriers provided for in the Treaty of Montevideo was undermined by being hardly automatic at all. In theory it was to lead to the elimination of customs duties and other restrictions within twelve years. But even if all the safeguard clauses were discounted, the mechanisms it established were not really suitable to reaching the objectives of the treaty. An 8 percent per annum reduction of the customs rates and other surcharges in relation to the weighted average applicable to nonmembers might have been possible by raising barriers against the outside rather than by reducing them within the area.

Even so, an exaggerated concern with reciprocity entailed having to negotiate product by product. As a result, and as is usual with this method, concessions tended to apply first to products which the countries concerned could not produce at all or which others were not likely to produce either. Liberalization of trade among the EEC countries had also been started in this way and would have been stuck halfway if the European Community had not invented an entirely different mechanism, the elimination of import quotas by enlarging them continually and in geometric progression to the point where they soon became ineffective so that they could easily be abandoned. Within the Latin American free trade area, some 11,000 concessions have been negotiated. They have managed to increase the share of trade within the area, at least in relation to the low point that it had reached in the early 1960s; it took a long time, however, before there was progress beyond the proportions of the early 1950s.

As of 1965, four of the most eminent Latin American personalities put forward more ambitious proposals. Their suggestions included general tariff reductions, maximum customs rates to be observed at different stages of integration, a gradual elimination of other restrictions, a common external tariff, and a general reinforcement of the institutional setup. The Conference of Presidents at Punta del Este, where the American president met with his Latin American colleagues in April 1967, came out firmly in favor of getting the integration process out of the ditch. But even so the date by which a full-fledged regional market would be established was postponed to 1985. Shortly after the conference a meeting of ministers to discuss common tariffs, a timetable for reducing customs duties, the gradual elimination of internal nontariff barriers, and special facilities for the least developed countries of the area, were not able to agree on even a single essential point. In 1964 it had been possible to consolidate concessions into a list covering 25 percent of trade; but it proved impossible now to extend this list to cover 50 percent. While the Treaty of Montevideo had set 1973 as the target date for total liberalization, it was now postponed to 1980; the annual rate for increasing internal preferences was reduced from 8 percent to 2.9 percent and the date by which a list of irrevocable common concessions was to be drawn up was postponed to 1974.

Is there a way out of this rut? In theory one could imagine that the industrialized countries might make access to their markets easier for Latin America and increase their financial contributions in proportion to the progress that the countries in that part of the world made towards integration. There would seem to be some logic in this sort of policy. After all, why open markets for industries whose bases are not wide enough to allow them to become competitive? Why give financial assistance if it doesn't produce the development for which it was intended? But this type of approach raises serious questions of principle, as well as material difficulties.

The attitude of the United States to Latin American integration has at best been ambivalent. Wedded for so long to the principle of nondiscrimination and to the most-favored-nation clause, it had a hard time overcoming its doubts on this score. As if high rates of protection, applied by each country individually, were less discriminatory and harmful to the development of trade than the formation of a group large enough to become an important exporter and as a consequence a larger importer. In fact the American position has changed; in the Alliance for Progress charter it has accepted integration as one of the objectives for Latin American development. When the American president participated in the second Punta del Este conference he declared that American policy now was to lend the strongest support to integration. However, in Latin America anything that comes from Washington is suspect. If the Americans had changed their attitude was it not because it corresponded to the interests of American firms in the region? Were they not preparing to rationalize their subsidiary activities in South America through a greater liberalization of trade? As for the Europeans, the Japanese, or the Socialist republics, their attitude is one of pure indifference. The Inter-American Development Bank, with an ardent supporter of integration as its president, has been able to devote part of its resources to financing investments of common interest. In this it has been supported by its major shareholder, the United States. It has also created an institute for Latin American integration.

But for this process to succeed the impetus must not come from outside, no matter how well meaning it may be. A fundamental question is involved here, for this area offers fertile ground in which to put into practice policies which would avoid relationships of dependence, not only with one or other major power, which in the Western Hemisphere would be the United States, but also with the industrialized world in general, even within a multilateral framework. The effort that must be made is to invent mechanisms which by their very nature will bring answers to the problems.

This requires that one start by reexamining the basic difficulties that integration raises for developing countries. Let them not fool themselves into thinking that European integration did not have major obstacles to overcome. It was only five years after the end of the most horrible of wars that this process managed to get underway. It too came up against irrational prejudices, vested interests, and bureaucratic habits. Nor can it be said that the European countries had more in common than other groups. They were divided far more than Latin America, by language, by a long series of wars and by conflicting hegemonial ambitions. Latin American difficulties, and those of other developing continents, are of a different order.

Difference in Size

One of these is the tremendous difference in size between countries. The European Community started off by bringing together three (now four) countries of comparable size with smaller ones which had already begun to form an entity among themselves. But between Brazil, Mexico, Argentina, and the rest of Latin America the disproportions are much greater; the same goes for Nigeria and the rest of Africa; and all the more so for Asia which has countries of all sizes, from the tiniest to the unwieldy mass that is India. In a sense the obstacle is more psychological or political than economic. In Europe the small countries are no less prosperous than the big ones—far from it! They are all firmly wedded to the idea of exports; thus their small populations or their limited size do not constitute inhibiting factors for their market. However in Latin America and elsewhere big and little countries have practiced industrial autarchy and have thus placed themselves in a situation where their lack of competitiveness could only limit their markets. Except for Uruguay, the smaller countries are, as a result, also those with the lowest level of income. These policies were not necessarily inevitable, but the question of difference in size had political implications. The smaller states have always feared competition as well as domination from the big ones. The largest countries, on the other hand, fool themselves into thinking that they have sufficiently vast internal markets; they are therefore not very seriously inclined to establishing cooperative arrangements with the smaller states—and the latter, in turn, fear that at any rate they would stand to lose more than to gain from such arrangements.

This difficulty is gradually being overcome in Latin America. The medium-sized states have formed a subregional group among themselves. It provides for trade barriers being eliminated more rapidly and more completely, and for the harmonization of the planning of infrastructure investment and the creation of new enterprises. Even though a Caracas conference failed to bring about any progress in establishing an overall free trade area, it recognized the compatibility of this Andean group with the general objectives of the Treaty of Montevideo. In other words, it was realized that a more limited but more tightly knit market could anticipate the eventual formation of a wider regional market whose prospects, for the time being, nonetheless remained rather slim. By bringing together a population greater than that of Argentina or even Mexico and a total production close to that of Brazil, this subgroup constitutes a factor of equilibrium since it tends to put the various negotiating partners on a more equal footing.

The other great problem, which was recognized right from the start was that of the considerable disparities in the level of development. However imperfect the measurement of per capita income may be, in Latin America it has been estimated as having a spread from 1 to 10 from country to country. Again one is bound to contrast this with the European Community members whose internal structures and standards of living were much more comparable—if one excepts for the moment the deep split between northern and southern Italy.

It is not that this basic problem of disparities has not been clearly recognized. Traditional theory held that disparities in development were spontaneously evened out by capital flows. It held that the profitability of investments was always higher in regions where there had been less previous investment. Thus, things were bound to come into balance. The unification of Italy, which made no allowances for the difference between an already well developed North and a very backward south, has shown how wrong this kind of reasoning was. After unification the south kept on getting poorer; it is only recently that there has been a deliberate effort to redress the balance. Another equally startling example is that of the United States after the Civil War. Up to then the South had been able to maintain some kind of balance with the North only because of slavery; when it, in turn, had to use free wage-earners, a deep gap began to appear. It wasn't until after the New Deal and the end of the Second World War and when traditional industries had started to move away from areas where labor was becoming scarcer and more expensive, that the South finally began to emerge from its relative underdevelopment. In other words, the same lags and disparities that accumulate on a world scale can happen just as easily within a regional market. The industrialized member countries could continue to draw ever-increasing advantages from their economies of scale and from what is generally referred to as "external economies," that is, a developed infrastructure for energy, communications, and manpower training. They could also continue to exploit the advantage of being closer to suppliers or customers. This kind of imbalance can only be overcome by deliberate and effective policies.

Regional disparities within the European Community have been tackled in two different ways. Firstly, by a general prohibition against any sort of subsidies, exceptions being made only for regions having particular difficulties either by virtue of their backwardness or because of their decline. The other means is the European Investment Bank whose funds are primarily, if not exclusively, destined to financing projects in the most retarded areas. A special arrangement, supplementing financial assistance, has also been made for countries like Greece and Turkey which are much less developed than the current members of the community but which will eventually join them. It provides for a much shorter period over which the core members abolish their protective barriers towards these less developed associates who are granted a much longer delay for reciprocity.

These are, in fact, the formulas which had been proposed from the start for Latin America, which were recognized in principle in the Treaty of Montevideo and later as regards Bolivia and Ecuador within the Andean group. The Inter-American Development Bank contributes to integration by virtue of the fact that it lends more to the poorer countries than to the less impoverished ones—and not only because of the common projects it finances.

One of the first projects which had been developed at the ECLA included a suggestion that each country spontaneously categorize itself as either "most advanced," "moderately developed," or "underdeveloped." Within each of these three groups protective barriers vis-a-vis all the member countries were to be eliminated according to different time-tables: ten years, fifteen years, or twenty years. This flexibility in eliminating protection would not only have been practical, but it would have reflected the particular interests of each category. Thus, only the most advanced would have been able to engage in joint development of heavy industry. Their protective barriers would have been lowered as a matter of priority on corresponding goods. The less advanced countries, not able to afford this luxury, would have kept the temporary advantage of importing machinery from the industrialized world. And the least developed would have benefited from a number of advantages, a combination of longer protection and more rapid access to the markets of others, which was an attraction for foreign capital. At the same time production machinery could have been imported without having to pay for the protection in the more advanced countries of the area.

However, in practice, Latin American countries have been reluctant to grant special privileges to their less advanced partners. Nor is the Central American Common Market or the Andean group enough of an answer to the difficulties which are due to disparities in size. While Mexico has declared its willingness to grant unilateral privileges to the small Central American republics, Brazil and Argentina have shown themselves to be much more preoccupied with their own development than with the creation of a Latin American market.

AN ORIGINAL SCHEME

Thus, if the integration process is to get moving again, something new will have to happen. New mechanisms will have to be invented which will give the countries concerned a clearer and more immediate interest in the preferences which they are to grant each other. At the same time, these mechanisms will have to take into account disparities in size and levels of development.

With the benefit of hindsight one realizes where the initial mistakes were made. They resided in the types of obligation that were required and in how reciprocity was interpreted. As in Europe, obstacles to trade were to disappear in accordance with a fixed timetable. While some exceptions were made for the least favored countries, the principle in effect among all the others was that concessions had to be equivalent. This kind of method cannot take into account the difficulties that these sorts of obligations can create for developing countries.

There are two reasons why European countries could undertake firm obligations (with limited escape clauses) and a fixed time frame for eliminating barriers amongst themselves. Firstly, because they had the means for coping with additional imports resulting from a common market; they could in effect count on the dynamism and the variety of their own exports. In other words, they could afford to take some risks. After all, chances were good that with a modified balance-of-payments structure overall figures would be increased and that while some changes would be largely unpredictable, a new balance would in fact emerge, sometimes, if necessary, through alterations in the exchange rate. The structure of the balance of payments did not constitute an obstacle to the elimination of trade barriers. Secondly, except in the field of agriculture, there was no real risk involved in granting preferences to one's partners. The supplies coming from one's neighbors, particularly in the machine industry, were perfectly competitive with those of the rest of the world. The economies of scale, specialization and pressures to modernize which came with the establishment of a vast market could only, therefore, lead to the increased competitiveness of the community's industries. There was no risk that their own production costs would increase owing to imports of more expensive or less well-made capital goods.

The situation of the developing countries is entirely different. For them, balance-of-payments difficulties are a perpetual obstacle—a veritable specter. And this explains why the various treaties signed in Latin America were filled with precautions and escape clauses. And yet, however complicated their provisions may have been, they have not enabled these countries to adhere to their timetables. Employment is a similarly preoccupying problem for these countries. There is, of course, some sense in thinking it better to have some of the working population badly employed than not employed at all. Finally, countries constantly threatened with an external deficit and having to worry about how to attract investment, tend quite naturally to save their currency resources for the purchase of machinery and equipment produced under the best conditions. They are more inclined to turn to the advanced industrialized countries for their capital goods than to take the risk of granting preferences in this area to their neighbors. This last difficulty, furthermore, cannot be overcome except through major joint projects which are very difficult to negotiate. One can try to spread around new industries or, in the case of complicated plants, to distribute them among the members that are parties to the agreement. But in the end the chances are that the result will be an expensive compromise rather than a rational division of labor. This way of doing things is closer to the kind of mistakes made by the Europeans in trying to set up organizations for space research than when they developed institutions for the Common Market.

The system that will have to be devised will, therefore, have to be such as to promote by its very nature the development of regional economic relations. It will also have to take into account the different types of difficulties that the various countries may encounter. And finally, it will have to avoid the obstacle of an external deficit. A scheme which tried to answer all these conditions has been developed for Asia. It could, perhaps, be applied to the integration of other continents and to renewed efforts in Latin America.

The basic idea is that increases in overall exports in any country of the region would be used to increase the share of its imports from countries within the region which have subscribed to the same obligation. The underlying principle and the immediate consequences are readily apparent. One starts from a genuine possibility of extending trade within the region, since the increase in regional imports is tied to the increase in world exports; that is, the means for the increase are available. An entirely different interpretation is made of the concept of reciprocity: it is no longer one of firm obligations with closely weighed mutual concessions which in the end are not adhered to. It is one of tentative obligations, but which will gradually become effective. No matter how slowly exports may increase, the increase will, nonetheless, take place and the process will, therefore, become self-accelerating.

A chain reaction is built in to this sort of process. When country A increases its imports from country B, the latter by the same token, increases its exports and can, therefore, in turn increase its imports from A, or C. A continuing process is thus started. In the beginning each country will be tempted to import that which it needs most and which offers the least competition to its own producers. But as the system develops, it has its impact on industry, it enriches trade, stimulates specialization and production on a larger scale.

The system also avoids having to define in advance the countries to which special facilities are to be granted. To date all systems of special preference aim at particularly small countries or, more obviously, at the least developed. In the mass of international documents on the subject a special case is also made for landlocked or sealocked countries. The advantage of the mechanism proposed here is that no classification of any sort is required. It is not absolutely certain, after all, that the least developed countries are those for whom increasing exports would be most difficult. The Central American countries, and also Peru, have been able to increase their sales much more rapidly than all other Latin American countries. Similarly, the export champions of Asia are four small countries, Taiwan, South Korea, Hong Kong, and Singapore.

Should some unforeseen difficulty arise in one or more of the countries concerned, they will not be saddled with any additional obligations; if their exports do not increase, they will not have to increase their imports from the other member countries. And yet they will continue to have the same opportunity as the others to find additional markets within the region. To give the whole movement a bit more impetus it could, moreover, include an agreement whereby if any of the countries, other than the large ones, do not manage to raise their exports, other members would give priority to reducing trade barriers, and hence to increasing regional imports on products which interest these countries.

A FLEXIBLE FORMULA

Once the principle is accepted, its application is relatively easy to imagine. A formula which puts the emphasis on increasing imports from parties to the same agreement has a double advantage: it puts the emphasis on the objective while leaving the techniques for attaining it quite flexible; it allows techniques to vary in accordance with whatever external trade control mechanisms exist in each country. Nor does any special exception have to be made to allow for purchases from non-members which may be considered important in some contexts. After all the acquisition of modern equipment and machinery should not be discouraged.

Yet how will an increase in this part of imports from other partners be defined? It will be subject to two conditions. Firstly the weaker such imports are to begin with, the faster they should be allowed to develop. Secondly, the chain reaction, which is the very essence of the proposition, must aim at a certain limit. Even the European Six, with their high degree of integration, had only about one-half of their trade among themselves; with enlargement this proportion can easily attain two-thirds, but this represents trade within a bloc which is by far the biggest commercial power in the world. It is clear, therefore, that the greater the number of members that are parties to the agreement, the higher will be the limit to which its internal trade can aspire.

There is a very simple formula for linking the rate of increase of imports from other member countries to the rate of increase of the overall exports of the country concerned. It has two coefficients. One links the two rates of increase: if it is higher than 1, the portion in question will increase proportionately more rapidly than total exports. A priori this coefficient could be unrelated to the number of countries, since the initial portion of imports would be that much weaker if the agreement is limited to a small number of signatories. On the other hand, the other coefficient, which determines the limit beyond which internal trade should not grow, must be related to the number of participants. The accession of new members would thus simply imply modifying this coefficient, that is, raising it as the number of members goes up.

The formula satisfying these conditions can be put as follows. Let P represent that part of total imports of a member country which comes from other member countries, at a particular time, at the beginning or later on. Let p represent the rate of increase there should be for this part. Let e represent the rate of increase of the given country's total exports. To link p to e there are coefficients a and n which will determine the limits of the mechanism as follows: $p=e(a-naP)$. When P reaches $1/n$, the term between brackets is nullified, and the increase required of p is reduced to 0.

It is clear, for instance, that if n is equal to 2, the limit to the group's internal trade will be established at one-half its total trade; if n=3 it will be at one-third; if n=10 it will be at one-tenth, etc. One could, furthermore, imagine that the value of a would be fixed at 1.5 or 2. On average, developing countries do one-tenth of their trade in their region; if their exports increased by 10 percent, their reciprocal imports should begin to increase by 15 percent or 20 percent, that is to say, rise to 11.5 percent or 12 percent. At the outset, the trend would accelerate rapidly, and slow down gradually as trade within the group became more substantial.

Having clarified these points the basic figures for the mechanism will have to be agreed upon. They will have to take into account the time lags involved in statistical data. There will have to be a simple formula: the most recent possible reference year and the rate of increase for total exports between that year and the most recent one for which figures are available. If there were a gap of one year between figures for export increases and regional import increases, this would not really create any fundamental difficulties.

One may well ask, of course, what the means are within each country for sticking to the agreement. It is precisely because of the variety of methods used in the different states that a common yardstick will have to be devised to compare the effectiveness of their mutual contributions. If their imports are done centrally by state institutions they'll increase them; if they apply quantitative restrictions, they'll increase the quotas. On the surface the problem appears more complex when more indirect methods are in use, such as customs duties, many different types of import surcharges, multiple exchange rates, etc. As there is no econometric measurement available—it would at any rate be very hypothetical for establishing a correlation between reducing protection and increasing imports—one can only proceed by trial and error, lowering barriers as long as the objective is not reached.

Some will no doubt maintain that in the more liberal countries, that is to say, those which regulate imports through customs duties only, there is no way to force importers to increase their purchases from member states. They forget, however, that after the European Community had rapidly eliminated its quantitative restrictions, it had no other means of increasing internal trade except through a progressive lowering of customs duties and the gradual establishment of a common external tariff. What is essential is that access concessions, once granted, be consolidated. Afterwards, one has only to rely on normal commercial behavior to develop increased trading relations, better communications and the development of sales networks.

There is no basic reason why this form of integration should be confined to the dimensions of a continent. The scheme that has been proposed here could very well be extended from one developing continent to another. The only condition is that there be no leakage in the system and that the increase of import shares only be allowed to operate in favor of countries which have accepted the same obligations. Thus the chain reaction will not be blocked; markets will expand, economies of scale will increase, and profitable forms of specialization will become more frequent.

Since the first UNCTAD, developing countries have been granted the right to give each other mutual preferences which would discriminate against the industrialized world. In practice such preferences have never really come into being. In the absence of any tangible advantage, each developing country considered that it would have entailed a sacrifice in favor of the others; it feared that it would, as a result, merely acquire inferior goods at higher prices. The type of agreement proposed here might get this kind of general movement going, since the countries best able to import would stimulate within their less privileged neighbors a trend which would be of benefit to them in turn.

A number of them have a certain freedom of choice. The biggest countries of any developing continent could decide to increase their imports from their smaller or less advanced neighbors and thus grant them certain preferences. In fact, considering the small amount of imports involved, such an increase could very rapidly be translated into a virtual elimination of the big countries' trade barriers vis-a-vis the small ones. It would be only normal, after all, if those countries which are on the verge of joining the club of modern economies made the same efforts for the less advanced countries as the underdeveloped world as a whole expects from the developed countries.

They also have another option. As they are already more industrialized than the others, these countries could choose to reduce their protection, and consequently increase their imports, to affect products which they might then develop in common. For example, in the sector of durable consumer goods or in that of capital equipment, where economies of scale are important. They would, in this way, find a more natural process by which to transfer from a purely national and autarchic industrial policy to the development of more competitive industries and export capabilities.

At any event, the scheme which has been described here does not fail to link the underdeveloped countries' mutual cooperation with that of the developed world. However careful or gradual it might be, the integration among developing countries must be allowed to proceed without stumbling at every step. It would be further encouraged by commercial concessions from the developed countries. Under this scheme, the benefits of measures such as reduced customs duties, eliminated quantitative restrictions, preferential access, would not be confined to a single country or a small number of countries. It would spread from one to the other, over all the countries of each continent or, more generally, over all of the Third World countries which will have chosen to unite for their own development.

Conferences are proliferating in and around the United Nations: in Bucharest on population, in Rome on food, in Lima on industrialization, plus the special sessions in New York on raw materials. The grandiose concept of a new economic order is slowly beginning to take shape in the positions adopted by the 77, in the charter of the economic rights and duties of the states, in the final declarations or action programs. Lip service is regularly paid to cooperation and interdependence, even between different economic systems; but the accent on national sovereignty, however exercised, remains strongest: over firms, threatened with expropriation, but above all over natural resources including territorial waters the limits of which are constantly being extended, in a world whose needs know no frontiers and are more and more unlikely to be met satisfactorily. Thus the dilemma of helping incompetent or oppressive governments or starving their countries remains unchanged. There are no overall programs to deal with the population explosion, few answers, save for some emergency stocks, to the threat of hunger. Commitments which have not been kept in the past are still being reiterated, such as the percentage of their national income which rich countries should earmark for aid. The illusion prevails that relations between the prices of what developing countries import and export could be settled by waving a magic wand: as though indexation could be limited to the sales of developing countries without applying to the same primary products supplied by the industrialized nations, so that the Third World might lose as much as it gains; and as though revenue did not depend as much on volume as on prices, and nothing can prevent sales from falling when demand slackens off. Copper and even oil producers know this through bitter experience.

For, even as good intentions are being written into international documents, as confrontations are toned down for the time being, the situation is worsening dramatically. The recession shows how the industrialized countries can always restore their balance of payments by selling a little more to the newly rich primary producers, but even more so through a fall in their imports. This is only a short-term solution which runs counter to the structural changes that are necessary in the long haul. The commodities and simple manufactures are hit hardest. In a word, the equilibrium reached by the industrialized world translates the whole surplus of oil producers into a deficit of the poorest countries. This is the worst possible outcome for it blocks any prospects for growth there where it is most necessary. And stability of the world as a whole is jeopardized; this imbalance, even with regard to marginal markets, threatens to perpetuate and multiply crises.

Thus the gap between economics and politics widens. The interests of the wealthy countries, both old and new, have proved to be more intimately linked than they had realized. For any recession has the effect of limiting the earnings of the oil countries, as well as indirectly affecting their rate of development. Here is a basis for a fruitful dialogue. In the long run as well: the producers and the consumers are equally concerned with conservation. At the other end of the spectrum, experience has confirmed that a rise in the price of oil or cereals, far from carrying along the other primary products, causes them to move inversely through the cutbacks in the levels of activity. Objectively speaking, there are conflicts of interest within the developing world, which will not always be veiled by aid from the oil countries to other primary producers.

Can these contradictions be overcome? Some steps which have been taken allow for a faint hope. An agreement was reached through a difficult process to recognize the complex links between energy, raw materials, and conditions for development. A decision has also been made to use part of the gold holdings of the International Monetary Fund for carefully planned sales on the free market, which would finance a supplementary aid to the poorest: the well-to-do in every continent have strictly limited that portion. The UNCTAD is working seriously on a scheme to stabilize primary products through buffer stocks, but, failing an agreement on the terms of an international monetary reform, the financing is not assured. The "third window" of the World Bank group, besides financing on normal or concessionary terms, would be based on borrowings from the countries whose exchange reserves have been swollen to be relent to destitute countries, at rates reduced through subsidies from industrialized countries. The implementation remains to be seen.

At least the European Community has moved ahead. Both in the number of countries involved and the extent of its provisions, the Lome convention goes far beyond the Yaounde agreements which it follows. This scheme is open to others besides the associated countries of Africa, the Caribbean, and the Pacific; it gives free access to the European market without requiring reciprocity; it provides compensatory aid to the countries concerned for a substantial fall in one of their essential exports. Such a principle should be generally accepted. It would mean that the richest countries give up the windfall which they would derive from lower prices at the expense of the poorest countries.

But nothing ample enough will be achieved as long as in the United Nations the emphasis remains on "nations" rather than on "united"; as long as the debates continue in terms of a transfer of power which is unacceptable to some and inaccessible to others; as long as countries will not in their daily dealings prove really aware of their interdependence, even in their relations with the weakest of them. Intentions are reaffirmed each time like litanies in which the layman is hard put to perceive progress towards agreement which has required so much diplomatic subtlety. One cheerfully underwrites hundreds of principles without ever taking actual steps to translate them into realities.

Action demands an entirely different approach: change should be focused on a few decisive points which carry along all the rest. Linking production plans and population prospects, setting criteria for aid, reforming transnational enterprises, managing the monetary system, restructuring production, transcending narrow national markets: all this means fewer, more closely interrelated goals, as well as more integrated instruments to achieve them. That is what is attempted in this book.

ABOUT THE AUTHOR

PIERRE URI is counsellor for studies at the Atlantic Institute for International Affairs, professor at Paris IX University and member of the French Economic and Social Council.

He has played an extensive role in French economic policy, in the construction of the European Communities, and as a consultant to international organizations in every continent. He is the author of numerous books and reports concerning integration, money, and development. He is also a noted columnist in France and in other countries.

He was a student at the famous Ecole Normale Superieure and obtained the highest degree in philosophy before turning to economics and politics.

BEYOND DEPENDENCY: The Developing World Speaks Out
edited by Guy F. Erb and
Valeriana Kallab

DEVELOPMENT IN RICH AND POOR COUNTRIES: A General
Theory with Statistical Analyses
Thorkil Kristensen

PATTERNS OF POVERTY IN THE THIRD WORLD: A Study of
Social and Economic Stratification*
Charles Elliott, assisted by
Francoise de Morsier

THE UNITED STATES AND WORLD DEVELOPMENT: Agenda for
Action, 1975*
James W. Howe and the staff of the
Overseas Development Council

*Published for the Atlantic Institute for
International Affairs*

DILEMMAS OF THE ATLANTIC ALLIANCE: Two Germanys,
Scandinavia, Canada, NATO and the EEC (Atlantic Institute Studies—I)
Peter Christian Ludz, H. Peter Dreyer,
Charles Pentland, Lothar Rühl

ENERGY, INFLATION, AND INTERNATIONAL ECONOMIC
RELATIONS (Atlantic Institute Studies—II)
Curt Gasteyger, Louis Camu, and
Jack N. Behrman

*Published for the Atlantic Council of the
United States*

THE FATE OF THE ATLANTIC COMMUNITY
Elliot Goodman

*Also published in paperback as a PSS Student Edition.

GATT PLUS—A PROPOSAL FOR TRADE REFORM: With the Text
of the General Agreement
                    Atlantic Council of the United States

U.S. AGRICULTURE IN A WORLD CONTEXT: Policies and
Approaches for the Next Decade
                    edited by D. Gale Johnson and
                    John A. Schnittker